THE ENVIRONMENTAL CRISIS●

●A HANDBOOK FOR ALL FRIENDS OF THE EARTH●

THE ENVIRONMENTAL CRISIS●

●A HANDBOOK FOR ALL FRIENDS OF THE EARTH●

EDITED BY DES WILSON
FOREWORD BY DAVID BELLAMY

Heinemann Educational Books
London · Exeter (New Hampshire)

Heinemann Educational Books Ltd
22 Bedford Square, London WC1B 3HH

Heinemann Educational Books Inc
4 Front Street, Exeter, New Hampshire 03833

ISBN 0 435 83943 8
ISBN 0 435 83944 6 Pbk

First published 1984

Library of Congress Catalog Card Number: 83-26448

Typeset and printed in Great Britain by
Biddles Ltd, Guildford, Surrey
Set in Plantin

Contents

Editor's Note and Acknowledgements

This is not an official Friends of the Earth book. To be precise, it is not published by Friends of the Earth and the views of the contributors are their own. However, all of the contributors have been involved with FoE over the years (and some still are), and in my capacity as editor, I have attempted to fulfil two objectives: first, to create a handbook for Friends of the Earth on the issues that concern the movement in Britain; and second, to introduce to others both those issues and FoE itself.

I would like to thank the Board of Friends of the Earth for their support for the project, and also the publishers, particularly David Hill. I thank each of the contributors for their co-operative response to my requests for their participation and the demands of deadlines, etc. Jane Dunmore's comments on the manuscript were invaluable and Susan Dibb and Patricia Simms, my colleagues at CLEAR, were typically helpful.

Finally, my fellow contributors and I gratefully dedicate this book to all the members of Friends of the Earth who in their daily lives and their work for FoE answer the call of the movement's American founder, David Brower:

> The resources that can be liberated without being exhausted are human spirit and love. They can bring the resolution. You can effect the decision. You have the gift. You can pass it on.

Des Wilson, May 1984

Notes on Contributors

DES WILSON is, at the time of publication, Chairman of Friends of the Earth in Britain, and also Chairman of CLEAR, The Campaign for Lead-free Air, and of the 1984 Committee for Freedom of Information. Born in New Zealand, he came to Britain in 1960, and was the first Director of Shelter, the National Campaign for the Homeless (1966–71). He has been active in other pressure groups, and is also a well-known journalist, having been a columnist on both *The Guardian* and *The Observer*, Editor of *Social Work Today* from 1976 to 1979, and Deputy Editor of the *Illustrated London News* from 1979 to 1981. His book *Pressure: The A–Z of Campaigning in Britain* is published at the same time as this book.

RICHARD SANDBROOK is Executive Vice President of IIED. He was a founder of Friends of the Earth in the UK, and Company Secretary and Director from 1970 to 1979. He has also been involved in Earth Resources Research, and the British Ecological Society, and has contributed articles to magazines such as *New Scientist* and *New Society*, as well as writing many papers on marine pollution and southern ocean issues.

CHRIS ROSE joined Friends of the Earth as Countryside Campaigner shortly after completing his chapter for this book in 1983. He obtained degrees in botany, zoology and conservation science at the University of Aberystwyth, Wales, and University College, London, and then spent four years studying lichen population ecology and recolonisation of London at Chelsea College. He has worked for a number of conservation organisations as a researcher, warden, and surveyor. In 1979 he was a founder member of the British Association of Nature Conservationists and edited its journal *Ecos*, and in 1981 helped found the London Wildlife Trust, for which he worked for a year as Conservation Officer.

DAVID BALDOCK first became involved with Friends of the Earth in its food campaign in 1976 and subsequently became a member of the FoE Board. He is Director of Earth Resources Research and works mainly on food and countryside issues. He is currently working on a report on European wetlands.

BRIAN PRICE is a freelance environmental pollution consultant who has advised Friends of the Earth on pollution matters since 1972. He is a frequent contributor to newspapers and magazines on the subject. He has recently completed a series of reports on lead pollution for CLEAR, The Campaign for Lead-free Air, notably on dust in school playgrounds, lead in tinned foods, and lead in paint. He is a member of two official committees dealing with the management of hazardous waste, and lectures part-time on the BSc Environmental Health course at Bristol Polytechnic.

CZECH CONROY has been fully involved in environmental issues for many years. He was Friends of the Earth's Energy Campaigner from January 1976 to March 1979 when he became Campaign Director. After 6½ years on the FoE staff he turned freelance environmental consultant in 1982. He has written numerous articles and reports on energy and other environmental issues. He has also given written and oral evidence to four parliamentary energy inquiries, and was the lead witness for the Council for the Protection of Rural England at the Sizewell Inquiry in July 1983. At present he is fulfilling a long-standing ambition to explore the wildlife and wilderness of South America.

MICK HAMER is a freelance journalist who specialises in writing on transport issues, most notably in *New Scientist, New Statesman,* and *The Observer.*

CHRISTINE THOMAS has been involved in the environmental and alternative technology movement over the past 10 years. Between 1973 and 1977 she worked for Friends of the Earth and Earth Resources Research, researching and campaigning on recycling and resource issues. More recently she has been working with the Alternative Technology Group at the Open University, on opportunities for community-based recycling schemes – and continues to do so, while also looking after her first child and helping to organise the NATTA Women and Technology Group.

WALT PATTERSON is a Canadian, resident in Britain since 1960. He was a full-time staffer with FoE from July 1972 to June 1978, mostly as the organisation's energy campaigner. He is now FoE's energy consultant. He has an MSc in nuclear physics; he is the author of *Nuclear Power* (Penguin) whose second edition was published in 1983. He is an editorial adviser to the *Bulletin of the Atomic Scientists*, and a frequent contributor to *The Guardian*, *New Scientist*, and other publications, as well as a broadcaster.

CHARLES SECRETT has been wildlife campaigner with Friends of the Earth since 1980. In that capacity he has organised national wildlife rallies, published many articles on wildlife and conservation, and frequently broadcast on the subject. He took a degree in English and American Literature, awarded honours, at the University of North Carolina. He subsequently worked as a residential social worker with children and has also worked as a gardener.

Foreword by David Bellamy

NO ONE ON earth need go cold or hungry. No one need die in pain. We *can*, after all, fly twice as fast as the sound of music, climb to the top of the highest mountain, dive to the bottom of the deepest sea, walk, ride, run and swim faster, jump higher and longer than ever before. People fly to the moon and our machines reach to the stars. Thanks to radio and television almost everyone on earth can enjoy the best of art, literature, drama and music, and nation can, at the flick of a switch, speak peace unto nation. All these things and many more have become possible in my lifetime. What a wonderful world!

But hang about a minute . . .

In that minute, 28 children under the age of five have died of conditions relating to malnutrition and environmental pollution, 70 hectares of forest have been destroyed, and 500,000 tonnes of good topsoil have been washed down towards the sea.

Think too on this . . .

● One third of the world's arable land is rapidly becoming a desert thanks to mismanagement, and it's not just happening in the developing countries.
● The cost of raising and distributing the crops which are being produced rises every year mainly due to the increased use and cost of fuel and investment in farm machinery.
● We are gobbling up the world's reserves of oil and coal at an ever-increasing rate. Some time in the not-too-distant future there will be none left.
● Atomic power has not proved to be the safe, cheap energy it was once cracked up to be. There is the growing problem of getting rid of the atomic waste in a place where it can do no harm. At the moment the real hot stuff is dumped in the sea.

And that is not all.

In the Persian Gulf, turtles, dolphins, even the sea cow, the rare strange creature that is reckoned to be the origin of the mermaid myth, die in a huge oil slick. Throughout northern Europe acid rain

– more acidic than lemon juice – is feared to be killing millions of fish. In the great oceans magnificent whales are hunted to their deaths – despite articulate opposition. In Britain the otter is disappearing, beautiful butterflies are extinct. Lovely orchids barely cling on. Radioactive waste, discharged from Windscale, is found in polar currents off Greenland. Great natural forests are torn down in South America, valleys are flooded.

And what of resources?

The chemical industries which provide the drugs, plastics, and many other things which make our modern way of life go round, need raw materials. In the main they are petrochemicals: what happens when we have burnt them all?

Clean rivers, clean air, clean beaches, clean estuaries overflowing with wildfowl and fish, nature reserves, sites of special scientific interest and national parks – fantastic things to have – were hard won by conservationists over the past 30 years. Many are now under threat by the mega-buccaneers of farming, forestry and development.

What is more, such destruction is often aided by government and EEC grants and subsidies. In my opinion, Britain should have a policy of self-sufficiency at least for our staple needs. Why should we go on producing butter and barley mountains to the detriment of our wildlife, soils and heritage landscape? Kinder use of the land is possible – thank God for our temperate climate. And our farmers can both conserve our cake and provide us with enough to eat.

We are told that thanks to robots and computers, we can all look to a future in which we will all enjoy a shorter working week and that we must be educated for leisure. Where will that leisure be spent? In sports complexes within concrete jungles set in a prairie farmscape – with no hedgerows and copses, no old quarries and small valleys with rivers and streamsides – straightened and groomed for ease of management rather than amenity or fishing. We are seeing the guts of our cities decay before us while developments, which could have kept them vital and alive, eat into the green belt areas where we used to walk the dog or take the family for a picnic only a bus ride away.

I can't put a value on a meadowful of flowers or a wood filled with birdsong.

Or on such glories as butterflies, frogs in the village pond, real ale in a non-plastic pub as the centre of a caring community.

Or on a view without buildings, a beach of clean sand and the sound of healthy, happy children.

I do know, however, that it has much more lasting value than an empty warehouse or factory block looking for work or an extra mega-buck blackening the economy.

We *do* live in a wonderful world – and we *can* keep it that way. This book will, I hope, help you to play your part.

PART **I**

● THE ENVIRONMENTAL CRISIS

DES WILSON

1 The environmental crisis

THE WORDS 'environmental crisis' appear together so often that they have in effect become one word. My dictionary defines 'crisis' as a 'turning point . . . a moment of danger or suspense'. Given that our planet has existed for hundreds of millions of years, the lifespan of one generation of its human inhabitants could be fairly described as a 'moment' and the word 'crisis' is justified by the overwhelming evidence that it is this generation – you and I – who are so careless of our habitat and so wasteful of its resources that we have become a threat to our planet and its multitude of other species.

Perhaps the best way to approach these matters is to project ourselves forward into the middle of the twenty-first century, or even the beginning of the twenty-second, and look at our contribution to human well-being through the eyes of our children and grand-children. Not only will their knowledge of history tell them how uncaring and selfish their forebears were, but their daily lives will reflect the price they will pay for our lifestyle today. That is, of course, assuming the human race will have survived at all, and that can hardly be guaranteed considering the world already possesses 50,000 nuclear weapons with a capacity to totally demolish the globe;

considering that by the end of this century, 90% of the population
will possess only 20% of its resources – a time-bomb of injustice that
too could one day explode with global implications; and considering
we are by our consumption and careless behaviour seriously under-
mining the earth's life-support systems.

If this appears to over-state the case, let's call a few witnesses:

The Brandt Commission . . .

> Few threats to the peace and survival of the human community
> are greater than those posed by the prospect of cumulative and
> irreversible degradation of the biosphere on which human life
> depends.

The Global 2000 Report to the President of the USA in 1980 . . .

> If present trends continue, the world in 2000 will be more
> crowded, more polluted, less stable ecologically, and more
> vulnerable to disruption than the world we live in now. Serious
> stresses involving population, resources, and environment are
> clearly visible ahead. Despite greater material output, the
> world's people will be poorer in many ways than they are
> today. For hundreds of millions of the desperately poor, the
> outlook for food and other necessities of life will be no better.
> For many it will be worse. Barring revolutionary advances in
> technology, life for most people on earth will be more precarious
> in 2000 than it is now – unless the nations of the world act
> decisively to alter that trend.

The World Conservation Strategy . . .

> Two features characterise our time. The first is the almost
> limitless capacity of human beings for building and creation,
> matched by equally great powers of destruction and
> annihilation. The escalating needs of soaring numbers have
> often driven people to take a short-sighted approach when
> exploiting natural resources. The toll of this approach has now
> become glaringly apparent; a list of hazards and disasters,
> including soil erosion, desertification, loss of cropland,
> pollution, deforestation, ecosystem degradation and
> destruction, and extinction of species and varieties.

The British Response to the World Conservation Strategy . . .

> During the past few decades, (our demands) on . . . natural
> resources, have risen to a scale that cannot much longer be
> sustained without exhausting vital supplies, dislocating the

delicate functioning of the biosphere and inflicting permanent and irreversible damage to this planet as the home of all life. . . . The gravity of this crisis is heightened by the fact that so many people remain unaware of it.

And so I could continue with quotations from one major report after another, for the environmental crisis is no longer the preoccupation of a few far-sighted individuals but is internationally acknowledged, its causes recognised, and the solutions already known. Sadly, knowledge has not led to action and the environmental crisis is but one reflection of an appalling absence of political will to face and tackle man's longer-term problems at source.

This book is intended to be an introductory handbook to British environmental issues, but we should look at our own problems in the context of the world environmental crisis, and even further, in the context of the priority agenda that mankind has to address – the genuine possibility of a nuclear holocaust, the huge north–south divide, and the environmental degradation and resource depletion that threatens to make the planet uninhabitable.

Why do environmentalists have to concern themselves with the peace issue? Firstly, because all human beings have to. Man's inherent violence and the escalation of his potential for violence must surely top the agenda of any discussion of the human condition. Second, because it is useless to spend a lifetime fighting for 101 policies to help sustain life on the planet, if just one act – the pressing of a button – can undo it all.

If one looks at the destructive potential of nuclear war from the point of view of the planet itself and our responsibility not only to this generation but those that will (or should) follow, then it is arguable that the real damage caused by a major nuclear holocaust would be far greater than its immediate death toll. As Jonathan Schell argued in *The Fate of the Earth*, we have to consider not only the immediate toll but 'how the ecosphere, looked at as a single living entity, with all forms of life dependent on it for their continued existence, would hold up'.

The Friends of the Earth in the US argue that 'from an ecological point of view, the war has already begun, as the mere preparations for it are causing illness and deprivation to humans, bringing harm to the planet's life-sustaining abilities and casting a deathly pall over life on earth. . . . Even if the shooting never actually starts, every stage in preparation for it brings danger to human beings and the planet.'

The Green movement, currently expanding in Europe, inspired by the success of the Greens in Germany, encompasses the nuclear threat and the environmental crisis within its list of priority concerns, and also the human tragedy of the Third World. Environmentalists cannot overlook the relationship between resource depletion and the desperate needs of the vast majority of the world's population who have to struggle to stay alive.

The World Conservation Strategy reports:

> . . . hundreds of millions of rural people in developing countries, including 500 million malnourished and 800 million destitute are compelled to destroy the resources necessary to free them from starvation and poverty – in widening swaths around their villages the rural poor strip the land of trees and shrubs for fuel so that now many communities do not have enough to cook food or keep warm; the rural poor are also obliged to burn every year 400 million tons of dung and crop residues badly needed to regenerate soils . . . thousands of millions of tons of soil are lost every year as a result of deforestation and poor land management.

The tragedy of the Third World is that in order to stay alive on a daily basis its inhabitants have no option but to devour and destroy the source of their own long-term survival and that of their children. As the late Barbara Ward wrote:

> One of the saddest of all metaphors is surely that of eating the seed-corn. Yet the inexorable pressures of population . . . or its resources are at the moment forcing hundreds of millions of people to do just this.

It must be stressed, therefore, that conservationists and environmentalists cannot dissociate themselves from these major issues as if they are separate and can be left to other campaigners or other movements; indeed, as resources become more scarce, or as the sense of injustice and desperation of the Third World becomes greater, these could become the causes of nuclear war in themselves.

How does one quantify the world environmental crisis? Its nature can best be determined by comparing the state of the planet with the aims of the World Conservation Strategy:

> (a)   To maintain essential ecological processes and life-support systems (such as soil regeneration and protection, the

recycling of nutrients, and the cleansing of waters), on which human survival and development depends;

(b)   To preserve genetic diversity (the range of genetic material found in the world's organisms) on which depend the functioning of the above processes and life-support systems, the breeding programmes necessary for the protection and improvement of cultivated plants, domesticated animals and micro-organisms, as well as much scientific and medical advance, technical innovation, and the security of the many industries that use living resources;

(c)   To ensure the sustainable utilisation of species and ecosystems (notably fish and other wildlife, forests and grazing lands), which support millions of rural communities as well as major industries.

At present, these objectives are not being met. In fact, we act as if our aims are almost the opposite. If we continue to degrade the land at the present rate, one third of all cultivatable land will be destroyed over the next twenty years. Arable land becomes desert at a rate of over 20,000 square miles every year. The proportion of land on earth that can be used for agriculture is just over 10%, small enough without its unnecessary decline. Deforestation and poor land management undermine the quality of the soil and reduce the protection of land; land loss and degradation represent a substantial threat to the survival of vast numbers of human beings. When we consider that in the last twenty years of this century the world's population is expected to increase by almost half – from just over 4,000 million to just under 6,000 million – the word 'crisis' begins to develop real substance.

The maintenance of forests, in particular tropical rain forests, is crucial, not only because they supply products such as timber but also because they have an effect on climatic conditions and even enhance the flow of clean water. They are also the homes of many thousands of species of animal and plant life. The probability, therefore, that the remaining area of productive tropical forest will be halved before the end of the century has serious environmental, economic and social consequences. What is happening to wildlife is equally disturbing. Excessive fishing and the 'developing' or polluting of fish habitats threatens the world stocks. We are each year allowing the disappearance forever of thousands of species of plant and animal life. Some 25,000 plant species and more than

1,000 species of animal life are now threatened with extinction. Furthermore, if you take into account small animal species – particularly invertebrates, whose habitats are being destroyed – there is a risk that between half a million and a million species will have been made extinct by the end of the century.

We are seriously polluting the air we breathe, the water we drink, and the soil in which we grow our food. As our dependence on chemicals has grown, so has widespread pollution. There are now 70,000 chemicals on the commercial market, and over 1,000 new chemicals are sold every year. Many are beneficial. Many more are employed with little or no knowledge of their potential effects and some are undoubtedly a threat to health and life. We are transporting around our globe hazardous wastes with inadequate control of their movement, storage, or disposal, and therefore adding further risks to the health of our generation and those to come.

And in developed countries we are producing technology and exploiting natural resources with no proper and sensitive planning of what we need to produce and what we need to save. As the American environmentalist, Barry Commoner, wrote in his book, *The Closing Circle*:

> Everywhere in the world there is evidence of a deep-seated failure in the effort to use the competence, the wealth, the power at human disposal for the maximum good of human beings. The environmental crisis is a major indication of this failure. . . . The environmental crisis is sombre evidence of an insidious fraud hidden in the vaunted productivity and wealth of modern, technology-based society. This wealth has been gained in a rapid short-term exploitation of the environmental system but it has blindly accumulated a debt to nature (in the form of environmental destruction in developed countries and of population pressure in the developing ones) – a debt so large and so pervasive that in the next generation it may, if unpaid, wipe out most of the wealth it has gained us.

As I have already stated, the facts of the environmental crisis are established and beyond argument. The world has been warned. It has also been shown that it has an alternative. That alternative does not require man to return to the Dark Ages, does not reject sensitive growth, does not treat all technology as an enemy and does not have to threaten the quality of life in its widest sense. It does call for controlled and sensitive growth, for technology to be the servant of human beings instead of their master, for an understanding that we all benefit when we reduce poverty, and for the adoption of known and proven alternative approaches based on renewable resources and a largely self-sustaining society.

This then is the international background to the environmental crisis in Britain. Of course, the problem assumes different dimensions when reduced from a global scale to a national scale, for just as poverty is relative, so is environmental deprivation relative. Clearly people in Britain are not attacking their environment in the way that the poor of the Third World do in order to survive. What we are doing, however, is contributing by our political policies and our individual lifestyles to both the international problems and a potential environmental catastrophe in our own country.

Britain's countryside, with all its historic beauty and diversity, is being steadily desecrated. Over 140,000 miles of hedgerow and between 30 and 50% of all ancient woodlands have been lost since the Second World War. More than 80 species of birdlife and 60 species of plant life and 40 species of animal life are so endangered that they have to be protected by law. Unfortunately, the places where they breed and feed are not similarly protected. We are losing a Site of Special Scientific Interest every single day. Yet, as Chris Rose demonstrates in Chapter 3, landowners and the bigger farmers have considerable power. With the Conservatives in power throughout the 1980s, they have been allowed to develop a system of public subsidy that would be laughed out of court if suggested for any other British industry. Those subsidies actually reward environmental damage.

The same Conservative administration has virtually declared war on public transport. The policies pursued have allowed the motor car to become totally dominant despite the fact that as a form of transport it is more expensive, more socially divisive, more energy-wasteful, more environmentally destructive, and unsafe. The scandal of British transport policy is described in Chapter 7 by Mick Hamer.

Our air, soil, and water is under constant threat of pollution. The complacency on these issues is astounding. Despite overwhelming evidence about the dangers of asbestos, the authorities have edged towards greater controls with exceptional caution. The decision to move towards lead-free petrol in Britain was only taken after a massive public campaign and in spite of Ministerial opposition. As for pesticides, it was possible in 1983 for the Prime Minister to say that 'There are no grounds for banning the controlled manufacture or use of 2,4,5-T', this only three years after the US

Environmental Protection Agency, having accumulated massive evidence, concluded: 'The quality, quantity and variety of data demonstrating that the continued use of 2,4,5-T contaminated with dioxin presents risks to human health is unprecedented and overwhelming.' Brian Price describes the 'invisible violence' of pollution in Chapter 5.

I cannot criticise British energy policy because there is no energy policy. We have a policy for electricity, coal, gas, and oil, but no overall energy policy. Each industry vies and struggles with one another for customers in the High Street and subsidies from the Exchequer. No utility has any incentive to promote conservation of energy with any vigour; rather, the incentive is to sell more appliances and more fuel. All the evidence that has been accumulated to suggest there could be financial and energy savings from a conservation programme, and also that such a programme would create over 150,000 unskilled or semi-skilled jobs, largely in deprived inner city areas where they are most needed, has been rejected. The Conservatives have set their hearts on a major nuclear energy programme that is unsafe, creates extremely serious problems of waste management and disposal, is vulnerable to exploitation by negative political forces, is uneconomic, and leaves an unacceptable legacy for the generations to come. The lack of imagination and the environmental hazard created by so-called British energy policy is described by Czech Conroy in Chapter 6.

The squandering of resources will be seen by subsequent generations as outrageously selfish. As Chris Thomas demonstrates in Chapter 8, a major programme of waste reclamation and recycling would conserve resources, and ultimately save money and the danger of environmental pollution as well.

Each of these chapters demonstrates the lack of vision of British political policies, their short-term nature, and the complete failure of our generation to fulfil its responsibilities to those who will follow. All political parties in Britain share responsibility for the crisis we face today in our countryside, the widespread environmental pollution, the dominance of the motor car, and our unimaginative energy and waste reclamation programmes. There is, however, no doubt that the Conservatives represent in the 1980s a major set-back for the environmental cause. Yet, as I wrote to the Prime Minister in my capacity as Chairman of Friends of the Earth in 1983:

. . . there is in our view no philosophical reason why this need be so. On the contrary, conservation and environmentalism should unite all parties. Indeed, one of the main strands of our thinking – that we should *conserve* resources – should be particularly attractive to *Conservatives*. We deplore waste, whether it be of the potential contribution of human beings, or of valuable resources, and would assume you would do so too.

Unfortunately, the Conservative administration of the first half of the 1980s has been characterised by short-term, blinkered economic thinking based on 'balance the housekeeping budget' principles, and has been seemingly unaware of, or impervious to, the fact that the house itself was falling down around it. There are many contradictions in this. After all, Conservatives talk most of the need to invest and save, yet unfortunately this philosophy is not extended beyond industry and the household budget to the well-being of the community as a whole. What are conservationists and environmentalists if we are not investors and savers? We wish to save crucial resources for our children and their children. We wish to invest to keep our planet habitable. Furthermore, even in strict economic terms, we make more sense, for we can see that wise expenditure now, and sensible conservation and environmental policies now, will cost a fraction of the economic (as well as social) price we will have to pay some day for their neglect.

Unfortunately, as I wrote to the Prime Minister, the Conservatives have an inclination to automatically support the commercial cause and the short-term and often selfish priorities of business, in preference to the long-term needs of the community. They have convinced themselves that what is good for business is automatically good for Britain. That, of course, is not necessarily so.

What is particularly sad is that the public appear to be ahead of the politicians on this issue. A major opinion poll in 1983 revealed that 50% of people in Britain believed that there was a serious risk of the human race using up all the world's natural resources. Well over 50% said they would support an increase in taxation to reduce wastage of resources. Over 40% said they thought environmental pollution was a major problem in the world today, and more than 50% included an attractive countryside and unpolluted atmosphere higher as amenities and facilities contributing to the quality of life than access to a car, sports facilities, leisure centres, and theatres. When the lead-in-petrol controversy was at its height in Britain another reputable public opinion poll revealed that 80% were prepared to pay more for their petrol to have it lead-free. There is, therefore, every reason to believe that there would be a positive public response to major programmes of environmental protection and reclamation, to activities to control pollution and conserve resources. Far-sighted and sensitive political leaders would mobilise that concern instead of blindly pursuing short-term policies that defy it.

Albert Schweitzer once said: 'Man has lost the capacity to foresee and forestall. He will end by destroying the earth.' It is a deeply pessimistic prediction. But it need not be so. Considerable numbers of people throughout the world have foreseen what will happen if we do not care for our planet and preserve it with love for our children. They have become what is known as the environmental movement and their numbers are increasing and their victories, at first local and small, have become larger. In Britain, too, it is estimated that over 3 million people support the many conservation or environmental organisations. Most of these, and undoubtedly Friends of the Earth, are not motivated by pessimism or the desire to be prophets of doom, but rather by anger at the stupidity of our behaviour and a conviction that there are practical ways of changing direction without enormous costs or adverse effects on the quality of life.

More and more people are beginning to respond to the challenge crystallised by the late Adlai Stevenson in 1965:

> We travel together, passengers in a little spaceship,
> dependent upon its vulnerable reserves of air and soil;
> all committed for our safety to its security and peace.
> Preserved from annihilation only by the care, the work,
> and, I will say, the love we give our fragile craft.
> We cannot maintain it half fortunate, half miserable,
> half confident, half despairing, half slave,
> to the ancient enemies of man, half free
> in a liberation of resources undreamt of until this day.
> No craft, no crew can travel safely
> with such vast contradictions.
> On their resolution depends the survival of us all.

This book is intended to be an introduction to environmental issues in Britain and a handbook for those who would like to become involved in Friends of the Earth or in other conservationist movements. The crisis and its causes are there to be seen, and the options also exist – options we can afford, options that are practicable, options that can enhance rather than spoil the best that life has to offer. The challenge and the task are clear. Time is running out, but still there is hope . . . if we change course now.

RICHARD SANDBROOK

2 Opening the environmental debate

IN RETROSPECT, THE Sixties were a golden decade. For many young people (including nearly all the founders of FoE in Europe) it was a time of radical if not slightly irrelevant student politics, an expectation of the good life, and a sense of modern technology working in harmony with man to his greater glory and betterment.

So, if life was so sweet, why was it necessary to create at the end of the decade a new and, for its time, radical addition to an already crowded environmental scene? With the power of modern technology to damage as well as to benefit mankind, the rising tide of population numbers, the potential for armed and nuclear conflict, and the naked facts of man and nature's predicament known the world over by way of the communications revolution . . . with these backdrops could any 'child of the sixties' sit back and enjoy the good life that was promised? Paul Erlich's joke of the time, that we were all travelling on the Titanic so why not go first class, seemed sick to many of the emerging students of the plateglass social science faculties. Something had to be done to offset the 'future shock', provide a 'blueprint for survival', ensure that the 'limits to growth' were recognised, and help to design a world where small was not only beautiful but possible. The notion of conservation alone was not enough. Environmentalism was to be the new creed.

The first OPEC oil shock was really the spur that moved the early environmental debate from the relatively trite concerns of returnable bottles and polluted rivers, etc., on to the bigger questions of sustainable resource use. Was mankind facing a series of resource limits? The public never really grasped this fundamental issue, since the media insisted in the early seventies – and sadly still does – on treating the oil shock as a fault of the oil sheikhs, and the environmental movement as being concerned with pollution and wildlife alone. The greater issues of a perhaps disappearing mineral resource base for economic activity, the environmental, social and individual stress imposed by vast population increases and the once-and-for-all time loss of our genetic resources seemed beyond the interest of the colour comic brigade. But these are still the issues that dominate the underlying environmental agenda.

It was Barbara Ward, writing in the early seventies, who put the ethic so engagingly:

> Alone in space, alone in its life-supporting systems, powered by inconceivable energies, mediating them to us through the most delicate adjustments, wayward, unlikely, unpredictable, but nourishing, enlivening and enriching in the largest degree – is this not a precious home for all of us earthlings? Is it not worth our love? Does it not deserve all the inventiveness and courage and generosity of which we are capable to preserve it from degradation and destruction and, by doing so, to secure our own survival?

Thus the foundation of all environmental concern is that mankind, now and in the future, can and must live sustainably and in harmony with the great beauty and natural wealth of the planet. A simple but powerful idea.

So what then constitutes the environmental concern of today set out in a form that engages the children of the eighties and beyond? There are two concepts that need to be put across in vivid ways to begin the testament.

The first of these is the notion of 'economic interdependence', as captured by the phrase 'Only One Earth'. We are now all interconnected 'earthlings', wired together so that we depend on one another to a fantastic degree quite unique in history. There is no place for nationalism as promoted by the radical left and right in these circumstances. The 'idol of the tribe' has no place in this age.

The question is, how do you make for stability in human systems when you have so much reliance on the next clan, tribe, nation or continent? Understanding how interrelations happen in nature may give insights for man on the basis of analogy and simplicity.

As a result of 'ecological' thinking, many now argue on the extremes of left and right (in environmental and traditional politics, but for different reasons) that we should set about undoing the great interconnected complexity we now live with. Go for stability by delinking ourselves. Reduce the number of independent or uncontrollable variables, for example, by cutting back on international trade that robs the poor (and creates unemployment at home). Move back to nature in small self-sufficient city states – bust up the power of the megalopolia and recreate a hierarchy of communes consisting of hunter/gatherers living within understandable and independent resource limits. The line of argument is reinforced by reference to nature. Short food chain systems are simple and arguably more robust: why not recreate them for man? Sadly, the solution of full-scale economic retrenchment is about as likely as the reversal of evolution in a tropical rainforest. Man just will not give up what he has already discovered – be it the telephone, jet airplane or television. We have to recognise interdependence and complexity in economic affairs as given, and work to make them stable (and hence sustainable) in terms of man and nature.

Ecological interdependence is also immovable. For example, it will take many years to see out the consequences of man-made changes to the chemical composition of the atmosphere. But you can be certain that a change for you is a change for me is a change for the next slug or panda. Ecological interdependence is certainly not reversible. So why then interfere with fundamental components of the biosphere such as air, water and genetic diversity without understanding what is changing and how fast it is happening? 'When in doubt – don't spill it out' became an early maxim of the environmental movement.

Understanding the notions of economic and ecological interdependence leads on to recognising that unbridled economic expansion is just too dangerous to have around. We must regulate the rate at which we burn off the world's carbon-based energy reserves, we must regulate the destruction of forest cover, we must regulate the introduction of toxic and carcinogenic materials into the environment. We must regulate the market-place. And so the 'idol of market' is dead too.

These two driving idols – of the market and the tribe – are

confronted full on by the notion of ecological and economic inter-dependence. But the idols are going to be hard to shift, as they were the basis of post-Renaissance man. It was the gradual breakdown of protective guilds and practices two centuries ago that liberated European man to an era of economic expansion. In just two centuries the new, free-market economics – of Adam Smith and others – resulted in a transformation of Mother Earth. The stimulus was competition and, as in nature, survival was achieved by the fittest. But a part of this growth by free enterprise was at great expense. First to nature: air was free, water free, natural resources there for the taking. The costs to earth were 'externalised' and dismissed (and still are in many ways). Pollute and get rich. Exploit nature and thrive. Second to man: exploitation of labour and territory was excused by the notion of trickledown wealth and 'economic' civilisation. Those who try succeed! Are we returning to these simple days?

Whilst this great free-market drive extended its tentacles into every facet of daily lives – from bread to house to health – so too the relentless drive of nationhood extended horizons and power. Expansion into empire was the dream of the newly industrialised world. Security of raw material supply, of future markets and of labour were satisfied by empire. Sadly this too had its costs that were easily put out of mind before the era of television. Nations who have want yet more, and, as two world wars and innumerous bloody campaigns will attest, the costs in human blood were high.

Post-war man has had to face these externalised realities. First came the reassertion of human rights and the liberation of empire. National self-determination re-established itself in a world of independent sovereign states. None must grow again at the expense of others. The birth of the United Nations and all the paraphernalia of protected national sovereignty was established as an inviolate barrier. With the recognition of human and national rights came the idea of international, national and individual welfare. The welfare state – extending to the international development agencies and the world of aid – began to protect human rights from the unbridled aggression of the marketplace. Then gradually came the accounting for nature's rights – and those of future human kind. We are yet to see satisfactory mechanisms for counting in these considerations, but if we accept the notions of economic and ecological interdependence, coupled with the protection of human rights and the conservation of nature, then the foundation stones of the environmental creed are in place.

The foundation stones are the easy part to define; what of the building itself? There are four interests that the environment debate is trying to reconcile within the framework of an interdependent world. They are those of the individual, the community, posterity and nature itself. As with all political movements, it is the reconciliation of interests that leads to progress and harmony.

The debate as to rights of individuals versus the community goes to the heart of traditional politics. The balance between equality and individual liberty is the cornerstone of the left and right debate. But where in that debate comes posterity? *In extremis*, what value does the capitalist or socialist put upon a wilderness, an endangered species, a magnificent tree? Do our children and our children's children have any rights in their debates? What of the nature of their inheritance? And where in that debate is the durability of nature questioned? The generosity of Mother Earth is always assumed.

The environmental ethic, which attaches the missing wheels, is only emerging with the post industrial age. And, as with all immature debates, the views are sharply polarised and the battle lines well drawn. In the green corner the ecocentric view prevails. Man is a part of nature. He must respect the natural order. He must integrate his purpose with nature's ways, not constantly strive to change nature. The weapons in the ecocentrics' armoury are 'uncertainty' – we just don't know what we are doing; 'extravagance' – why waste resources when we could conserve; 'arrogance' – how dare we undo what has taken millenia to construct? In the red corner stands the technocentric. Man is apart from nature. He has the tools of science at his command. He can monitor change, assess its impact, control adverse effects.

Just as the ground rules are still in the definition stage, so too are the battlefronts. Confusion abounds as inconsistencies, stupidities and half truths are revealed. Can we really deny emerging nations the right to change their landscapes as we have done? Surely their forest lands are there for them to use as they choose? Do whales have feelings and should these be considered? What then of fish, or shrimps or plants? Agriculture has always changed the landscape; why stop now? If oil is running out, why not go nuclear? – it is safer than digging coal! And so on.

So much of the debate is negative because of polarisation, and thus misses essential points. Taking care of nature's interests does not mean returning to nature. It means that the processes of nature must be preserved: the carbon cycle, the water cycle, the nitrogen cycle and so on. Evolution itself is put at risk. Conservation is concerned with nature's processes, preservation only with the end result. Environmentalism is about conservation, not only preservation.

Taking care of man's future generations is an argument over future choices. Posterity for posterity's sake is not the argument: but keeping future options open is. How can we know what the consequences of losing a species are? How can we allow all habitats in intensive agricultural areas to be destroyed when we don't fully understand what it is we are destroying? Lord Ashby, in his search for defining nature's interests, compares our polluting a river with allowing a valuable work of art to decay. It amounts to negligence. An abrogation of our duty to future humankind and the process of nature itself.

Arguing for a more sensitive development process is not necessarily an argument for no development. It is about durability in development, and the consideration of nature's time scales. Why kill the goose that lays the golden egg? Why not feed it, nurture it, protect it? The conflict between the high discount rates of the economist and the lower rates of nature must be reconciled. Why destroy a forest land for today's buck, only to result in a desert thereafter? Why overfish today and leave no stock for the future?

Thus the environmental debate has far to go. The mechanisms by which we account for nature, for posterity, as well as for equality and liberty, are hardly started. The reconciliation of these interests is a dynamic process. Defining ground rules now is futile and self-indulgent. But what must be considered soon by the economists of this world is how much they take for granted, and how much less they will be able to take for granted as our numbers relentlessly grow. Mankind as a whole must see the danger signs of assuming too much of nature. What we do now is not sustainable. The soil will go, the fresh water will dry up, the fish will vanish, the air and climate change, and evolution reassert itself with yet more virulent viruses and vectors. These considerations must form an essential part of the body politic.

Thus we move to the prescription stage. What is it that should guide our policies – as of now?

The first problem concerns attitudes. We are all in great danger of becoming bored with the restatement of the problems on a global scale. The slogans, catch words and metaphors are beginning to lose their appeal and effectiveness. How small is beautiful? What future shock and when? Limits to whose growth and of what kind?

As the clichés become media events in themselves, perhaps unwittingly we have obscured the pluralism and the complexity of the real issues of population growth, resource-management and the inequitable division of wealth. (Harland Cleveland, 1981).

Many have come to see that it is time to start work energetically on some of the components of the solution, rather than merely to talk of the problems.

But there are still plenty who ignore problems overall, or find excuses to do nothing dramatic or comprehensive. Again, Harland Cleveland has said: 'Governments, as we all know, are too responsible to take the responsibility for change'. This seems to be particularly so in the UK where it is a tradition of our establishment to react quietly to problems rather than to charge ahead with highly publicised new initiatives. Thus, our civil servants, politicians and academics have hardly been notable for leading the crusade of global environmental concern. It may well turn out to be a case of the tortoise and the hare, for once the nation is mobilised in a particular direction it is enormously resourceful, consistent and practical. But even so, it does seem to take an inordinately long time first, to convince UK Governments and commercial interests of many of the trends and, second, to act. To take contemporary examples: the condition of the ozone layer, acid rain in Europe and lead in the atmosphere from vehicle exhausts. In each case the UK has been reticent and accordingly misunderstood by its neighbours.

But by arguing consistently we must set about changing the attitudes of 'establishment' Britain. When the issues relate to more distant lands the arguments needed to justify action and expenditure become all the more difficult to muster. Why, for example, should the UK Government care about the destruction of the rain forests? After all, the erosion of the world's genetic stock has little direct impact on the UK's economy. Why should the taxpayer be asked to pay for clean water supply in the Third World when there is a clear reluctance to invest in our own municipal system?

It is too easy to blame the politicians and their civil servants. Democratically-elected politicians respond to expressed political pressure and, while there is some public concern for the plight of the world's poor – and probably far more for the plight of the world's flora and fauna – there is hardly an overriding clamour for political and administrative change on either ground. Even the environmentalists have traditionally been far more concerned about domestic issues: for example, the health risks of nuclear power as opposed to the millions who already die of water-borne diseases. The chosen environmental *cause célèbre* is rarely, if ever, global and seldom based on a rational analysis of environmental, economic or strategic risks. Making the link between environment and development into a thesis for sustainable development is our second goal.

Part of the difficulty (and this causes the polarity referred to earlier) is that it is often impossible to assess the risks that some of us fear. Our understanding of the state of the environment, most particularly in the developing countries, is very scant indeed. In the expert assessment of the state of the world's environment in 1982, performed for the United Nations Environment Programme (UNEP), the conclusion is blunt. They suggest that, on a world scale, we know much about atmospheric trends (CO_2, ozone, turbidity and precipitation chemistry), of food contamination trends (heavy metals, organochlorines) and that we are reasonably informed about the distribution and flow of fresh water. The state of forest cover is becoming better known (but is still an area of some dispute); regionally, we have a good idea of the condition of certain seas, of atmospheric pollutants and their movement, and of land-use patterns. But there are vast areas of ignorance. For example, there is little reliable data on the pollution of the oceans, and on the condition of ground waters. Our understanding of desertification rates, the condition of rangelands, farmlands, and other major land-use categories is patchy and incomplete.

In contrast, information on human activities, including those that affect the environment, is better. Information on food production, fishery statistics, trade statistics, and information on energy production and use are extensive. Demographic data are quite good, but disease data are often poor. At a national level, and perhaps even more importantly at a local level, our understanding of environmental change and the rate at which it is occurring is very poor indeed.

The obvious conclusion is that too little is being done to establish the hard facts and then to bring the issues onto the political agenda in a form that is not just a meaningless restatement of 'global this and that'. Issues, trends, policies and actions now have to be defined in a disaggregated form and in a way that does not result in helplessness and despair. Strident idealism and exaggeration are of little use once the work has begun. So elucidating the facts is our third goal.

At Stockholm in 1972 the environment debate went international. Without doubt much has changed since and we should capitalise on it. New insights and attitudes have emerged that could make a great difference to our future, and events have not been insignificant either. For example, during the decade the number of States with governmental institutions dealing with environmental management has grown from 15 to 115 countries (1980). Much domestic environmental legislation has followed. At an international level, the UNEP has been established and it has tried, and to an extent succeeded, in carrying forward a range of substantive environmental reforms. The EEC has recently agreed its Third Environmental Action Programme which includes radical proposals for environmental coordination in Europe and an important chapter on environmental policy outside the Ten. The OECD has begun to debate many of the issues at a ministerial level. The nine leading multilateral lending banks have signed a far-reaching declaration on the environment. Many, if not all, of the bilateral aid agencies are trying to integrate environmental considerations into their procedures. The world has seen a series of high level UN conferences, all relevant to the issues: for example the Population Conference, the Food Conference, the Human Settlements Conference, the Water Conference, the Tropical Rain Forest Conference, and the New and Renewable Energy Conference. All were pregnant with worthy environmental recommendations for the world community to act upon. But, most significantly, there is beginning to be a fundamental shift in global political attitudes.

In 1972, many influential people in the developing world considered that the environment issue was, amongst other things, yet another attempt by the North to impose trade barriers, by way of expensive pollution controls, on the South. Indeed many in the North did regard environment as being synonymous with pollution. But gradually these two views have shifted.

In Nairobi, at the tenth anniversary session of Stockholm (1982), not one developing country raised the pollution issues in these terms. Without exception, Governments expressed concern at the damage being done to their countries' environments which adversely affect their development and the condition of many of their peoples' lives. They called for help.

The North has also been jolted into considering the longer-term by the publicity given to, for example, the outer limit theories of the computer modellers – in particular by *Limits to Growth* (1973). The 1972 Organisation of Petroleum Exporting Countries (OPEC) action caused many to consider our economic dependence on raw material suppliers. The sub-Sahelian drought vividly brought the plight of destitute people to our television screens. The rising carbon dioxide levels and the condition of the ozone layer have caused much comment about climate trends and artificial changes to the biosphere. The Global 2000 report certainly raised the debate in parts of the US Government machine.

In short, many Governments and, more relevantly, many more people have come to realise that we cannot isolate ourselves from the widespread destruction of humanity's resource-base that continues largely unabated. As a result there is perhaps more of a consensus on how to proceed into the last few years of this century than 10 years ago. There is certainly more public appreciation of the issues. The fourth job is to build on this progress. We must not get down at heel about the changes that have occurred.

Finally what is the present consensus? Who knows? Six points of agreement seem to emerge:

(a)   Slowing down the rate of the world population growth is an essential goal to solving so many of the problems of developing countries and regions. It is difficult if not impossible to achieve this without an improvement in the wealth and welfare of the world's poorest peoples. Development is the priority for them.

(b)   Sound development is not necessarily slowed down by environmental concern but it is demonstrably made more lasting and durable by way of it.

(c)   The consideration and integration of natural constraints within economic plans for development is not easy, but is an essential step in the longer-term. Short-term economic benefits have to be weighted with longer-term environmental costs.

(d)   The unacceptable position of the world's poor is amongst the most serious global environmental problems we face. Poverty (particularly amongst the rural poor) is a powerful agent of environmental destruction.

(e)   The developed world must adjust its economy to much less wasteful, resource-intensive and damaging activity, whilst the developing world must respect the carrying capacity of its natural systems.

(f)   The world now desperately needs skilled manpower, and money to move these ideas of sustainable development forward into substantive action.

The environment is not the only concern. Central to this chapter is the concept of sustainable development underpinned by 'sound natural resource-management'. The two are mutually dependent. The UK is, and should be, concerned with both. The rationale for the UK's concern with both is based on the concept of global inter-dependence: moral/economic/strategic. Our involvement with both sustainable development and natural resource-management should be manifested in terms of our domestic policies and by how we interact with the world around us. That is the challenge of the next decade.

PART **2**

● THE ISSUES

CHRIS ROSE

3 Wildlife: The battle for the British countryside

'This is politics: not conservation'
Caufield, C. of the Wildlife and Countryside Bill

OF ALL THE events that have affected Britain's countryside in recent years, there was one – the passing of the *Wildlife and Countryside Act* in 1981 – which even the most distinterested observer must have found hard to overlook. While it achieved little or nothing for conservation on the ground, the Act changed everything in the politics of the countryside. Indeed it politicized nature conservation itself, a loss of innocence which many conservation groups have yet to come to terms with. The Act therefore provides a convenient pivot for this chapter.

It is customary to fix a time and place to such things, so for what it is worth, historians might like to note that it was probably on a warm evening in June 1981 that British conservation lost its political virginity. The venue: in or near Committee Room 14, House of Commons, Palace of Westminster, London, SW1.

The *Wildlife and Countryside Bill* had started life in the House of Lords and progressed through its Second Reading in the House of Commons to the Standing Committee which comprised twenty-one hand-picked MPs. Along the way the Bill had proved much more controversial than the Government had expected (in the end it attracted a record 2,300 amendments) and it was now bogged down in further wrangling as the Government systematically reversed the few pro-conservation amendments that had been pushed through against Government advice in the Upper House.

For the dozen conservation lobbyists and representatives of voluntary wildlife groups who regularly crowded on to the narrow wooden bench along one wall of Committee Room 14, the scene and proceedings had become depressingly familiar. Facing each other across panelled oak woodwork and seated on slightly more comfortable green leather furniture, the Government and Opposition MPs argued each point interminably. In a wooden courtroom style press box, a journalist from a Sunday newspaper scribbled notes. Opposite, and furthest from the environmentalists with their assortment of jackets and T-shirts, was another box where a small coterie of dark-suited civil servants rested bulging brief-cases on their knees, equipped with notes for the Minister on the habits of redshank, acreages of heathland affected by fire or agriculture, or the possible number of bulls you would meet on footpaths.

As the proceedings wore predictably on, with the Government mindful of private commitments to the farming and landowning lobby, exercising its in-built majority on each issue, conservation observers grew increasingly despondent about securing any sort of improvement to the key section (Part II) dealing with means of protecting habitats. Ironically, it was only by accident that the Government had had to make any proposals for habitats at all. The Conservatives had been instrumental in the demise of the previous Labour Government's Countryside Bill which had fallen with the previous Parliament in April 1979 but they had come to office to find themselves saddled with an obligation to enact new conservation leglislation by April 1981 because Britain had signed the EEC Birds Directive on April 2nd 1979 (*Directive on the Conservation of Wild Birds 79/409*). The Wildlife and Countryside Bill had been laid before Parliament in October 1979, after hurried consultation and behind-the-scenes agreement with the Country Landowner's Association (CLA) and the National Farmers Union (NFU) but had been badly delayed from January 1980 and was not introduced to the Lords until November 1980, in which time conservation had quite fortuitously become suddenly much more controversial.

As if this wasn't enough, Conservatives such as Lord Craigton and Lord Sandford had teamed up with Opposition Peers such as

Labour's Lord Melchett who was also involved with most key wildlife and countryside organisations, to inflict some well-publicised and embarrassing defeats on issues such as Marine Nature Reserves, funds for maintaining landscape features and promoting conservation on farms in National Parks ('the Sandford Amendment'), a ban on Sunday shooting, and legal protection for the redshank, curlew and bar-tailed godwit. (For a detailed account see Cox, G. and Lowe, P., further reading.) Conservationists had also been keen to secure better protection for all Sites of Special Scientific Interest (SSSIs) and for moorland in National Parks. In the Commons' Committee Stage, however, Government discipline was stricter and the Minister (Tom King) was proving unbending on key issues.

Indomitable Opposition MPs such as Tam Dalyell and Peter Hardy amazed conservationists with their ability to talk with apparent interest, for hours on end, about the plight of Wiltshire's downland or the interesting features of the common scoter, and for honour's sake the Minister engaged them in battle on interpretation of statistics of habitat loss, the pros and cons of planning control, compulsion or the 'voluntary approach': issues on which the Government had in fact no intention of conceding a jot. Then the Opposition received an unexpected opportunity, as the Government ran short of time.

While the Committee Room debates centred on nightingales, disappearing hedgerows and medieval meadows, outside and a few miles south across the Thames, Brixton was burning. In Toxteth too there were riots. Labour MP Tam Dalyell wrote not long afterwards:

> Crudely put, if the Opposition did not get what it wanted for honourable reasons . . . we would talk past mid-day each day of the report stage, and lose the following day's Parliamentary business – which would be the Finance Bill – or, in all probability, pressing discussion on the riots. Faced with this *force majeure*, Government business managers would happily give us Sandford, SSSIs, Moorland, footpaths and marine reserves.

So, where reason, popular support and the interest of the media had failed to win conservation any real concessions from the Government, party-political opportunism did. It was a striking political education but why was it necessary? With over three million people paid-up subscribers to one environmental group or another, and with a *Daily Telegraph* Poll showing 77% support among the public for tougher conservation laws, the wildlife lobby might seem to have done remarkably poorly in Parliament. The explanation for this is largely historical, and lies in the long period of almost total political inactivity among conservation groups from 1947 to 1979.

The Ambridge Dynasty: 1945–1979

In 1943 a committee of the British Ecological Society noted:

> In the post-war planning of agriculture . . . it has been proposed that hedgerows and small copses should be largely eliminated . . . such a policy if applied to extensive areas would largely destroy the beauty of much of the English lowlands. It would destroy the main habitats of many of our most cherished wild flowers and also the breeding places of most of our small birds.

Unfortunately, the foresight of a few scientists and others was quickly swamped in a wave of post-war enthusiasm for farming, which had just saved Britons from starving at the hands of the U-boat menace. Agriculture was 'a good thing' and while food was still rationed, wildlife was not.

So it was that when planning development controls were laid down in the 1947 *Town and Country Planning Act* they excluded agriculture (and forestry) as a form of development. Nor did the 1949 *National Parks and Access to the Countryside Act* provide national parks or SSSIs with any other protection against untoward agricultural or forestry change: such sites might, by dint of sympathetic planning, be protected from roads, houses, gravel digging, airport buiding, or even from cricket pitches, but not from drainage, ploughing or afforestation.

And to sow the seeds of disaster more firmly yet, the 1947 *Agriculture Act* introduced a remarkable principle which was to set conservation and agriculture on an eventual collision course. Marion Shoard in *Theft of the Countryside* (see further reading) has described it thus:

> 'For the first time in history', announced Tom Williams, the Minister for Agriculture, as he introduced the Bill, 'the farmers will be able to plan ahead with certain knowledge of market and price. . . . I fully believe that this machinery for providing stability represents the most far-reaching step that has ever been taken in the history of agriculture'. The means of price support chosen in 1947 was the system known as deficiency payment. The Government guaranteed farmers minimum prices for the main farm products and these were set at levels

which would ensure that farming was profitable. As long as the market price was higher than the guaranteed price, then the market price was what the farmer received, but when it fell below the guaranteed price, the farmer received a 'deficiency payment' from the taxpayer to make up the difference. At the same time, food imports were subjected to tariffs and quotas.

It seemed like a good idea at the time.

The deficiency system of support continued until the early 1970s, when Britain's agricultural bureaucracy phased in the EEC system. This had begun as a system of ensuring a living wage for those Continental farmers whose basic methods – such as horse-ploughing teams and crop rotation – had changed little for decades or centuries. Its effect was to encourage limitless increases in production, making every acre which was 'lost' to a wood, hedgerow or marsh, a lost profit. With such encouragement, agriculture as a whole grew larger, with greatest expansion in the most profitable, mechanised, intensive and industrial types of agriculture. Driven by the incentive of guaranteed profit, agriculture's coming technological revolution was to eliminate traditional landscapes wholesale, sweeping away the hedges, valley meadows, old woods, footpaths and copses to be found on small mixed farms, and with them most of the families who had made and used them.

And as Britain became steadily more urban and suburban, and people's direct contact with, and understanding of, agriculture and the countryside diminished, so a romanticised arcadian image of agriculture formed and became fossilised in the public mind. It owed more to the script-writers of the BBC rural soap-opera *The Archers* than to a changing reality, and was exploited to the full by the NFU. By 1980 Marion Shoard was to write:

Urban based society feels it does not understand the country-side. We tend to believe that the people who are best equipped to decide what goes on there are the farmers who run it. Farmers benefit from a prejudice built into England's cultural tradition which insists that the countryside breeds more whole-some people than the towns and that, therefore, farmers are the best custodians of the countryside we could possibly wish for. This idea is fostered by everything from breakfast cereal commercials and children's books to radio and television series. . . .

In the early 1950s the bucolic vision of a countryside stocked with wildlife and yeomen farmers milling about the fields around a thousand Parishes of Ambridge, at least had some truth to it. The SSSI system and National Nature Reserves network were intended to be built up gradually to take stock of the rich variation still remaining in Britain's semi-natural habitats. For the rather esoteric purposes of teaching ecology, as well as wider though ill-defined purposes, a 'representative sample' of Britain's habitats was to be selected and designated, site by site. As agriculture seemed unlikely to change, the system was academic rather than protective by design.

The countryside of the early 1950s still contained many habitats essentially unaltered for centuries or even millenia. Despite the effect of wars and early trends in forestry, much of the woodland remaining was ancient, dating back far beyond the Norman Conquest. Most individual woods were isolated from one another and had existed as discrete places with names and histories, throughout the Middle Ages. Woodland management such as coppice-with-standards (coppice involves regrowth and periodic cutting back from 'stools' or stumps) had been continuous for up to 4,000 years. Under such conditions, not only had many of the species from the primeval 'Wildwood' survived, but man's activities had left a tapestry of earthworks, banks and markers, pollards, tracks and other signs on the woods which, superimposed on the natural disposition of tree stands, merited Richard Mabey's description in *The Flowering of Britain* (see further reading):

> These old woods, weather-beaten, hard-worked, spun about with legend and history, each one stocked with its own exclusive cargo of flowers, are life-rafts out of the past.

Rarities such as ghost orchid or red helleborine had survived adapted to particular conditions – of light, shade, soil, leaf-fall or moisture – or in particular types of wood – ash, hazel, sessile oak on Welsh cliffs, Caledonian pine, lime in Lincolnshire, wych elm. So also had the common species: primrose, dogs mercury, woodcock. Conservationists understood little of such woods' history at the time but they did set about 'representing' the rich range of variation in the SSSI system, although it only ever touched a tiny minority.

If power saws were unknown in the woodlands of the day, so were tractors a rare sight, chemical fertilizers scarce and chemical sprays almost unknown in the grasslands and fields of the early 1950s. The range of permanent grasslands was almost as rich and bewildering as woodland: from the chalk downs of the south and east, where pasque flower, lizard orchid, yellow-wort and adonis blue butterflies were still found, to the equally alkaline northern limestones where species such as globe flower and teesdale sandwort prospered, reminders of an Arctic influence; through fine river-silt hay meadows with yellow-rattle and snake's head fritillary, to clays of permanent pasture supporting green-winged orchid, adders tongue fern and twayblade. Up to a hundred species could be found in a square metre of even quite average ancient grassland, a self-sown mixture gradually established over thousands of years, including plants and animals whose natural homes ranged from sea-cliffs, to dunes, forests, river-banks and marshes.

Wetlands, heaths, peat-bogs and upland lichen-heaths, water-meadows, a hundred different sorts of lakes and streams, Devon banks and Midlands village greens, commons and mountain pastures: all these had survived centuries of man's use because agriculture, forestry and even land drainage and river management had remained ecologically gentle. There were 300,000 horses in 1950 (greatly outnumbering tractors), getting their form of fuel from the acres of traditional hay meadow which were still a common sight. Even in arable areas, while the cornflower and corncokle were dwindling, children on a spring walk could still rely on finding frogs in the ponds which flanked almost every field. Otters were regarded as common and were hunted from Norfolk to Cornwall, from Dumfries to Kent.

In the mid-1950s, agricultural change gathered momentum. 1,200 km of hedgerow were being removed a year using capital grant aid from the Ministry of Agriculture, which was also promoting the use of more chemicals. Nevertheless conservation concerns remained fixed firmly on traditional enemies. The 1954 *Protection of Birds Act*, for example, was a milestone of wildlife legislation and a famous victory for the lobbying effort of the RSPB (then with 7,000 members) but was concerned with persecution and egg collecting, not the loss of habitats. Soon, however, Britain's finest birds were losing their eggs to an altogether more sinister adversary than even the most manic oologist.

In 1955 several localised incidents of bird-deaths were reported in areas where heavy applications of organochlorine pesticides, such as DDT, were being made. Then in 1957 the British sparrowhawk population crashed, never fully to recover. The same year thousands of fish-eating grebes died at Clear Lake, California in the USA, where DDT had been used against mosquitos. In 1957 returns from otter-hunting in the agricultural areas of England began to show a sharp drop; in 1958 it continued and in less than ten years, contacts with otters halved. This was later traced to infertility caused by pesticide residues, washed from fields into rivers, and passing up the food chain to the otter. The same thing was happening in the case of birds of prey, this time causing egg shells to be excessively thin and break in the nest. By 1963, only 44% of the peregrine falcon population was still breeding and the Scottish population of golden eagles, one of the most vital in Europe, had crashed.

Rachel Carson's book *Silent Spring* was published in 1962 amidst uproar from the world's agrochemical companies. Yet the growing wave of disquiet in Britain was channelled not into a direct challenge to the planning and encouragement of the land-use revolution that was affecting the countryside, but into a prolonged attempt at accommodating modern agriculture within the aims of nature and countryside conservation.

A voluntary ban was introduced on some pesticides, under the far from satisfactory Pesticides Safety Precaution Scheme. In 1963, National Nature Week was followed by the first of a series of 'Countryside in 1970' Conferences, which with others of the time, actively sought a union of interests between farming and wildlife and amenity conservation, while concentrating attacks on the perceived threats of motorways, urbanisation, car-bound recreation, over-population and impending, if vaguely defined, 'global catastrophe'. Meanwhile a very real local catastrophe was proceeding effectively unchecked.

Agricultural production increased by leaps and bounds. By 1966 the grain harvest had trebled. More land had been brought into production. For example, of the 800,000 km (an area of 160,000 ha) of hedges that had criss-crossed and wound their way over the English landscape in 1947, grubbing-up had accounted for 8,000 km a year up to 1963. When in 1964 conservationists met in York to discuss the urgent need for chalk grassland conservation they decided, typically, to concentrate on buying more nature reserves (though funds were not sufficient), and not to press for controls over agricultural development. A year later, an economist at the influential Oxford Farming Conference was urging Lincolnshire farmers to rip out 48 miles of hedgerow to save up to £1,440 a year (1965 prices) – just one of many cases. Similarly, from 1953 to 1976 the use of chemical fertilizers increased eight-fold, and by 1975 farmers had twelve times the number of pesticides available to them in 1944.

At the same time the countryside emptied of people at work. The enormous increases being claimed in 'efficiency' were not just due to greater yields per acre, but also per man. From 1948 to 1979 agricultural workers left the land at over 7,000 a year, the total falling from 563,000 to 133,000. They were replaced by machines and energy, in the form of oil, fertilizer, chemicals and electrification of dairies, pig units and battery farms, which did not appear in the measurements of 'efficiency'. In fact, calculations by energy consultant Gerald Leach suggest that the horse-based intensive rotation agriculture of 1950 probably produced a ratio of food energy gained, to energy put in, of around 1–200:1 (primitive agriculture being c. 15–20:1). By the 1970s this had climbed to over 1,000:1 – but if the hidden subsidy of fuel, electricity and petrochemicals was accounted for, the 'profit' of 1,000:1 turned into a loss of 1:2. Far from becoming more efficient, British agriculture gobbled up more energy than it produced. (In his book *Fuel's Paradise* Peter Chapman notes that this makes a mockery of the oft-heard suggestion that a 'green revolution' could feed an enormously increased world population if the developing nations emulated Britain's agricultural system: there simply wouldn't be enough energy available as fuel.)

The energy subsidy of agriculture prompted the ecologist H. T. Odum to remark that 'man no longer eats potatoes made from solar energy; now he eats potatoes partly made of oil'. In addition, the ever increased horsepower of machinery makes it literally easier to flail down a hedge, put up an earth dam, grub out a wood or plough on steep slopes. A modern tractor might plough up forty acres in a day where a horse team would have struggled with one. Laying drains under fields, for example, is such an energy- and power-demanding task, that until the 1960s the last major burst of drainage activity in many areas had been with prisoners' labour during the Napoleonic Wars. But mechanised methods cut the 'real' costs of drainage by 50% between 1954 and 1976. In 1945, just 12,000 hectares were field drained (pipes laid underground) in England and Wales; by 1974 the area had risen to 103,000 hectares and was still increasing at 12% a year.

Throughout the sixties, conservation groups fretted about the expected impact of tourism, recreation and cars in the countryside. An age of leisure, rather than unemployment, was in prospect. Symposia and seminars were held on 'public pressure', and a whole new pseudo-science of recreation ecology grew up, with gadgets such as trampelometers for the tedious demonstration of the obvious. In the end, with some careful management and establishment of projects such as Country Parks set up by the Countryside Commission via Local Authorities (under the 1968 *Countryside Act*) the threat of public pressure proved largely chimerical. However, the fear was enough to forge an alliance between nature conservation groups (though not of course recreation groups) and the farming and landowning interests, in the face of an imagined invasion of the countryside.

This encouraged the wildlife groups to develop further their latent streak of elitism and xenophobia, which only helped the farming and landowning lobby and hindered conservation when it finally came to mobilising popular support. The 'keep out' school of thought was particularly influential among the middle-class County Naturalists Trusts (now widely renamed Wildlife Trusts) which were establishing many small nature reserves and emulating the scientific trappings of the Nature Conservancy (renamed the Nature Conservancy Council in 1973).

The tendency to dogmatize the scientific jargon and practice of ecology as a code of pseudo-values was also to prove a serious mistake. Reference to the 'scientific value' of a site, or even of a species or individual plant or animal, was enough to justify keeping people out of nature reserves, and by association, to suggest that keeping people out of the countryside was itself good conservation and desirable. It hijacked the values of ordinary people with a genuine interest in nature, substituting a structure of expert opinion which was more susceptible to the machinations of developers and organisations such as the NFU and CLA (with 'ecological consultants' to provide 'objective scientific evaluations') than to the goodwill of families who visited a beauty spot or who loved bird-watching on a holiday beach. It was what zoologist C. S. Elton must, thirty years earlier, have had in mind when he warned the fledgling Trusts against becoming 'a new feudal aristocracy of the scientific age'.

In retrospect it is easy to see that, apart from largely cosmetic tree planting schemes, the protracted attempt to persuade farmers to voluntarily undertake significant conservation measures was doomed from the start. The 'three Cs' ethic, espoused at the 'Countryside in 1970' Conferences, was finally given the ultimate stamp of establishment approval when it was adopted as the main plank of proposals (for maintenance of the status quo) put forward by the civil service Countryside Review Committee in 1974. In reality, though, 'consensus, cooperation and compromise' was a very weak straw blowing in a powerful wind of agricultural change. Nevertheless, the placebo effect of the consensus ethic was remarkable, acting on conservation's concerns like a soporific drug. 'The Countryside in 1970 Conferences set us back a decade' remembers ex-FoE Wildlife Campaigner, Angela King.

In fact, although by the early 1970s wildlife groups were increasingly anxious about species vanishing from the countryside, they could, with a few exceptions, provide little hard evidence. Reports produced in 1968 and 1973 pointed to a dramatic decline in the population of the otter. Numbers had halved across England and Wales; fewer than a quarter of suitable river sites in the traditional strongholds of Norfolk and Suffolk held any otters at all, and the entire East Anglian population was estimated at under forty pairs. Habitat destruction, as well as DDT toxicity, had taken a severe toll. Only one river of any size (The Wye) remained in a basically natural condition in the whole of England and Wales. Everywhere, drainage, canalisation and 'river improvement' eliminated the habitat, not only of otters, but of hundreds of once common species, such as purple loose-strife, sedge warbler and kingfisher. In this parlous state the otter was more susceptible than ever before to the disturbance caused by otter-hunting (with dogs), despite a supposed voluntary ban on making kills since 1968. Even this did not stop one hunt organiser writing to his members:

> Help me to kill a few otters this season and I think that next year we will shake the pessimists by showing just how many there are about.

Throughout the early 1970s, studies of habitat and species-decline trickled into print. In 1970, botanist Frank Perring showed that 50% of the plants which had declined or become extinct since 1800 were victims of agricultural change, compared with just 9% and 7% affected by the traditional enemies of collecting and urbanisation. In 1972 J. Relton found that of every 100 Huntingdonshire ponds present in 1890, just 74 remained in 1950, and a mere 44 in 1969. In 1973 Carys Jones published a study of Dorset downland showing a decline in area from an index of 100 in 1793, to 55 by 1815, to 38 by 1972. However, such studies took data from such a long time period that they obscured the more intensive and irreversible nature of modern change, which involved chemicals and wholesale changes to soil structure which had never featured, for example, in the cycle of fallow and hay meadow ploughing in the eighteenth century. Published in dry scientific papers, or planning documents, these esoteric studies entirely failed to excite the public imagination. Habitat destruction remained a 'threat' appreciated only by a small number of outspoken ecologists.

For the main part, wildlife groups concentrated their efforts on establishing nature reserves, creating a cosy, cloistered world of sanctuaries. Only token efforts were made to influence the fate of the wider countryside, through weak and ineffectual groups such as the FWAG (Farming and Wildlife Advisory Group) set up in 1967. FWAG promoted the consensus ethic wholeheartedly, and was enthusiastically supported by the Ministry of Agriculture, the CLA and the NFU. FWAG's key supporters included people such as Derek Barber, an agriculturalist who in the mid-sixties had co-authored an influential farming text entitled *Farming For Profit* which had encouraged habitat destruction. In 1970 he edited a volume entitled *Farming and Wildlife: A Study in Compromise*, and was later made Chairman of the Government's Countryside Commission. Whatever its intentions, FWAG and similar projects were utter failures in terms of halting habitat destruction. They encouraged complacency about the general countryside among conservation groups, and let the farming and landowning lobby exploit the Dan Archer image of farming still prevailing in the media mind, to suggest that planting a few trees in field corners, or creating a new farm reservoir with sloping instead of vertical banks was going to replace any wildlife and landscape lost to expansion and intensification. It was an arid argument, ignoring the historical importance, and as it turned out, the non-recreatable properties, of ancient woods, hedgerows, meadows and of course, landscapes, lanes and views.

Heads in the sand, conservationists busied themselves with acquiring nature reserves. By 1975 the RSPB had 48 reserves totalling 32,000 acres, and nearly 200,000 members. The Trust's reserves increased from less than 50 in 1960, covering under 4,000 acres, to 850 covering 58,222 acres by 1975. The official NCC's National Nature Reserves numbered 99 in England and Wales (cf. 47 in 1963) with another 41 in Scotland, in all some 282,980 acres. Yet these apparently impressive totals often indicated nothing more secure than lines on a map. Of the 3,209 SSSIs designated by 1975 (819 for their geology, the rest biological) many had not been visited for years, due to NCC staff shortages. As late as 1979, two-thirds of all National Nature Reserves were not owned, but merely leased or run under 'management agreements' which enabled owners to get tax advantages. When, in the late 1970s, many leases came up for renewal, fears surfaced that rapidly-rising land values would make them prohibitively expensive. The huge cash-flow through the agricultural industry, and the guaranteed profit that an agricultural field might represent, had made agricultural land a seller's market. In the jargon, it was capitalisation of the farmer's cash flow.

This sure-fire investment also attracted institutions into the best land markets, where by the late seventies they became significant landowners on Grade 1 and II land. It encouraged amalgamation of farms and farm-managers with the sole object of giving a fixed rate of return to investors such as pension funds. Farmworkers made redundant by mechanisation had no chance at all of entering such a market for land. High land values also drained the resources of conservation groups; in the absence of any other strategy they were forced to try and purchase any land they really wanted to conserve.

The only notable piece of wildlife legislation to become law in the 1970s also failed to address the central problems for the natural environment, concentrating on the relatively insignificant effects of collecting, hunting and persecution rather than changes in land-use. This was the 1975 *Conservation of Wild Creatures and Wild Plants Act*, which merged several draft measures (such as a proposed rare plants Bill and a Bill for endangered reptiles), and gave piecemeal protection to a sprinkling of the most obscure and attractive threatened species. One, the large blue butterfly, had been declining for decades, as its specialised downland habitat went under the plough. By the mid 1960s only four colonies remained, and with their populations isolated, the slide to extinction was inexorable: despite last desperate attempts at captive breeding, in 1979 only 22 adult large blue butterflies flew over the last chalk turf plot and they left no descendants. Other species on Schedule 1 of the 1975 *Act* included the greater horseshoe bat, smooth snake, cheddar pink, lady's slipper orchid (of which just one plant survived in the wild) and ghost orchid. Many were typical ancient-habitat species, co-evolved with others in the stable ecology of long-lived environments, the temperate equivalent of tropical forests. The large blue, for example, depended not just on a particular food plant but also on an ant. The lady's slipper orchid needs a particular fungal species for its seed to germinate.

While the 1975 *Act* conferred protection on these species if they became rare enough to be in danger of extinction due to 'taking or killing', it also added the extraordinary proviso that such actions were to be allowed if 'carried out in accordance with good agricultural or forestry practice'. The tone of the Act reflected the failure of conservationists to confront the continuing expansion of agriculture (the 1975 White Paper *Food from our Own Resources* called for continued growth in production of 2½% a year).

Two years after the 1975 Act, the NCC published Norman Moore's study *Nature Conservation and Agriculture*. The report was something of a milestone, being the last widely-supported attempt to find common ground with modern agriculture, and a compromise solution. Its logical calls for reform of MAFF's agricultural advice system, of capital grants and the need for a national land use strategy, were politically hopeless, and caused little more than eyebrow twitching in Whitehall. In truth, the report should have prompted a scandal but it did not: for it detailed previously unknown losses of habitats and species; but was still couched in the cloying terms of consensus, compromise and cooperation. The beautiful blue pasque flower, for example, had declined to occupy a mere two dozen areas; marsh clubmoss, a plant of lowland wet heaths, was reduced to 53 locations from over 150; and the marsh gentian had declined by over 50%. The recorded range of one of Britain's most attractive butterflies, the silver spotted skipper, had shrunk by two thirds since 1950. In the same years, the chaffinch, once the commonest bird in the country, had become quite scarce in arable eastern England. Nature reserves, the report pointed out, occupied only 0.8% of Great Britain, and only 1% of the more fertile land. Even if all conservation sites – including the 3,535 SSSIs of the time – were to be conserved, only 4.1% of Britain's land would be set aside or acceptable for wildlife. The 142 flowering plants and ferns confined to ditches, hedgerows and other habitats still occurring on ordinary farmland, could still be lost.

The agriculture report's author commented:

> The decline is serious; it is occurring throughout the lowlands and the more fertile uplands of England, Wales and Scotland, and, taking Britain as a whole, the rate and extent of change during the last 35 years have been greater than at any time in history.

But the report lacked a sense of shock, anger or outrage. Not surprisingly, it made very little difference to MAFF, CLA or NFU. The newspaper *Farmer's Weekly* remarked complacently in 1978:

> Landscapes will change as they have done to meet the needs of succeeding generations. And future conservationists will inherit something new and interesting to protect.

The Exmoor Principles

The drive to expand Britain's agriculture affected National Parks along with everywhere else. At the scenic and ecological centre of Exmoor National Park in south-west England, a core of heather moorland was reduced from an extent of 59,000 acres in 1947 to

47,000 in 1976. Species such as the merlin were threatened but the most vociferous opposition to the ploughing-up of moorland came not from wildlife groups as such but from campaigners for access and amenity. (In fact the falsity of this historic divide, which has proved such a handicap to environmental campaigning, was illustrated in the case of Exmoor by the fact that the SSSIs, valued moorland views and walking country largely coincided.)

What particularly galled conservationists was that the National Park Authority, whose prime concerns were supposed to be with the care of a national asset, was itself conniving in, or at best turning a blind eye to, the ploughing-up, reseeding, and conversion to intensive pasture of the moorland. From 1962 to 1977 conservationists fought a running battle with the Authority, whose first National Park Officer was a retired major-general farming on the Park's edge, and whose key members were farmers and landowners. (For a detailed account see Anne & Malcolm MacEwen's book *National Parks, Conservation or Cosmetics*). The Authority never tried to prevent MAFF from ignoring its general responsibility to have due regard for the need for conservation (applying to all public bodies under the 1968 *Countryside Act*), and never used the Section 14 power of that *Act* to secure a management agreement with a farmer, paying him not to plough up moorland. At the suggestion of the NFU and CLA, which were keen to avoid compulsory measures, a number of farmers cooperated in notifying the Authority of proposed plough-ups but no proposal was ever stopped as a result.

By 1977 things were so bad that the Countryside Commission made the first ever use of its powers to 'report' the Authority to the Minister, and the Ministry of Agriculture and Department of the Environment subsequently appointed Lord Porchester, a former Chairman of the Association of County Councils, to sort out the mess. He reported quickly, recommending that MAFF grants for reclamation (moorland destruction) should cease in a key central area and Moorland Conservation Orders would be servable by the Authority, binding in perpetuity, for which owners would receive a lump sum in compensation. As well as simply prohibiting certain operations (e.g. ploughing or reseeding) the Order would specify certain types and levels of management to retain the ecological and visual character of the site (e.g. restrictions on fertilizers, recommended levels of grazing) as well as allowing for access. Lord Porchester also suggested conservation agreements, whereby farmers could get public money for non-agricultural measures needed to conserve the moor.

The importance of the Exmoor case and Porchester's recommendations (themselves adaptions of existing schemes to a small extent) is that the way they were received – by Government, Opposition, conservation groups, the NFU, CLA, individual farmers and landowners – has had a great influence on the *Wildlife and Countryside Act* and its implementation. The basic disagreements over private and public rights that lay behind the Exmoor arguments also have much wider and directly contemporary significance.

As it was, the Department of the Environment's lawyers were instructed to write the Porchester proposals into a draft Bill (the 1978 *Countryside Bill*), including conservation agreement finance of up to 90% and compulsory Moorland Conservation Orders, under which once-and-for-all compensation would be paid according to the difference in the capital value of the land before and after the Order was made. The Bill however was doomed, as, although the Committee stage was completed, it was one of the measures to which the Conservative Opposition refused to lend support when Parliament closed for the 1979 General Election, and when Labour lost, the Bill was buried too.

The Tory hostility was unsurprising, since, in line with the NFU and CLA, they had objected to the principle of restrictions on farming. Furthermore, the NFU had objected to the once-and-for-all method of compensation and even if there were voluntary (gentlemen's) agreements, the NFU wanted farmers to get an index-linked sum, calculated from the loss of potential profit that might have been made if reclamation had gone ahead. The difference might at first sound a fine one but the consequences are enormous. Under the once-and-for-all system, Porchester worked out that the nation would need to find nearly £1m to fund all Orders for the whole moor. Yet, under the annual-loss-of-profits system proposed by the NFU, the cost would be £0.38m *every year*, spiralling upwards from 1974 prices. The two systems rest on different premises: Porchester assumed that as with planning in towns, it was in the public interest that an owner's development rights be bought out (this is not to say that development would *never* be allowed, merely that it might not be). In contrast, the NFU assumed that farmers should always have the right to do whatever they liked with any of their land in order to maximise profit (unlike an owner of urban land) and that even where a farm owner or occupier entered into a voluntary conservation agreement, he would need paying off *as if* the land was being developed for maximum profit. The MacEwens comment:

From the point of view of the landowner or farmer this would turn the 'waste' of Exmoor into an excellent investment. From the point of view of the taxpayer it could be seen as a bottomless pit.

When in spring 1973 the Conservative Government of Mrs Thatcher reached office, the Moorland Conservation Orders did not appear in the new Bill, although a reserve power to make notification of reclamation compulsory does exist. Instead, the Government fell back on a purely voluntary approach and negotiations took place in autumn 1979 between NFU, CLA and the Exmoor National Park Authority, with the DOE, MAFF and Countryside Commission observing, to agree financial guidelines, which eventually gave farmers a choice between 'once-and-for-all' or annual-loss-of-profts. These too were to resurface after the *Wildlife and Countryside Bill* debates, as the basis of the guidelines for that *Act*.

Debunking the Scientific Gamekeeper

In spring 1980 Sir Ralph Verney, an ex-President of the Country Landowner's Association, a landowner with estates in Anglesey and Buckinghamshire, a farmer and forester, was appointed to be Chairman of the Nature Conservancy Council. At the time when the CLA and NFU were doing their utmost to constrain any pro-conservation regulations in the draft wildlife bill, it was a remarkable piece of effrontery. Verney had a long track-record of involvement in conservation issues. As an England Committee member of the NCC at the time of the Third London Airport inquiry, he had argued that the airport should go at Maplin (in spite of NCC officers' concerns for the rare geese there) instead of Cublington, very close to his mansion at Claydon in North Buckinghamshire. His appointment was strongly criticised by a number of conservationists, all the more so when it was revealed in *The Sunday Times* that he had opposed designation of Sheephouse Wood, on the family estate, as an SSSI. Conservationists who had visited the wood feared it could go the same way as nearby Charndon Wood, another ancient wood which had been dug up for clay by the London Brick Company, with which the Verneys had connections.

Similarly, concern was mounting over other appointments to conservation's key quango posts. Farmers, foresters and landowners dominated the Countryside Commission and the Nature Conservancy Council. Forestry interests exercised a particularly direct control over NCC's enfeebled policy on lowland woodland conservation and forestry. NCC Council and key National Committee discussions thus featured individuals such as forester Jean Balfour (also Chairman of Countryside Commission for Scotland), Lord Dulverton (forester, landowner and leading light in the Timber Growers' Organisation), Sir David Montgomery (Chief Forestry Commissioner), and Viscount Arbuthnott, who, as Verney's deputy, was also a landowner and at various times a President of the Scottish Landowners' Federation and the Wildfowling Association of Great Britain and Ireland (WAGBI: now renamed British Association for Shooting & Conservation). In an era of dawning realisation that farming, landowning and forestry interests were basically antipathetic to conservation, conservationists were right to question whether such people were most suited to further the wildlife case. When it came to a crucial vote of the *Wildlife and Countryside Act*, Viscount Arbuthnott was to vote against conservation groups' advice, but with the NCC and Government.

Fortunately, just as conservation was beginning to recover some of the sense of purpose it had so sadly lacked in the 1960s and 1970s, a book appeared which revitalised the movement and gave it more conviction. As an ex-rock writer better known as the author of *Food For Free*, Richard Mabey was unabashed by the prevailing convention that nature conservation and scientific 'rural resource management' were necessarily equivalent, and clearly did not share the view that a technical solution could be found to the conflicting needs of conservation and modern agricultural, water or forestry development. His book *The Common Ground: A Place For Nature In Britain's Future* quickly became an anthem uniting almost everyone with a genuine desire to see their country conserved. Mabey's arguments were personal, but they were appreciated not in spite of but because of this.

Mabey pointed out, in reference to the poet John Clare's compelling account of countryside change, that:

> Clare was describing a transformation in the fabric of rural England in terms of the destruction of specific features by identified agents. Yet they are not just particularized, they are *personalized*. Those were *his* trees, *his* brooks, *his* moles – not by virtue of ownership, but of *familiarity*.

As an approach it spanned the gap between whales in far-off seas, the greenhouse effect and the World Conservation Strategy, and the primrose copse 'cleared for wheat with such speed that I wondered if my memory of playing in it as a child was a fantasy'. Site of Special Scientific Interest, observed Mabey, really meant 'of interest to a particular kind of scientist'. As a call to arms, it worked: even groups such as the RSPB began talking of 'holding the line' instead of compromise.

It was undoubtedly instrumental in focusing the attention of environmentalists on what they could do about valued parts of their own environment, and provided reasoning that any politician could follow:

> . . . though we are now beginning to realize the wider importance of the natural world – even the small fragments remaining on these islands – I do not feel that this makes the *personal* case for nature conservation any less important. There are, after all, many millions of people who have such a case.

Farming Exposed: The Fall of Dan Archer

In October 1979, days before the delayed first debate of the *Wildlife and Countryside Bill* was due to begin in the House of Lords, Marion Shoard published her critique of agriculture *Theft of the Countryside*. Few books can ever have had a more direct effect on a political debate.

The farming press and the NFU raged in complaint but she had expressed and clarified a mounting wave of concern, shared by millions of people. Reviewers loved it: 'A good story . . . the facts are plain . . . the system is insane' proclaimed *The Times*, while another wrote: 'Marion Shoard has decided, at long last, to break through the stifling consensus and spell out the truth about the scale of financial support given to agriculture and the purposes to which money is put'.

For the first time in decades, the debate over the countryside and its resources was brought down from the atmospheric heights of abstract demands for a rural land use strategy, viable populations of species and ecosystem function, to specific and highly tangible questions such as whether or not an individual landowner, farmer or forester should get public money to change an ancient woodland to a spruce plantation, or plough up a marsh to grow rape or barley. Mabey's ethical renaissance had re-established the personal argument in favour of conservation – which opened the way for having to conserve every tree, brook, or bank for which there was popular support – and Shoard's political analysis made the agricultural bureaucrats, farmers, foresters and landowners, and their political lap-dogs, personally answerable for land-use change. The gloves were coming off.

Shoard marshalled the facts to show how rapidly the country-side was changing. In England and Wales from 1946 to 1974, 120,000 miles of hedges were lost; 45% in Norfolk for instance, and even a third in Worcestershire. Of woodlands, 16% of deciduous woods in west Cambridgeshire were cut down to make way for arable cropping from 1946 to 1973, while almost a third of the broadleaved woodland in central Lincolnshire was converted to conifer plantation. Even in Devon, a fifth of native woodland was lost between 1950 and 1970. 73% of the healthland along the Suffolk coast was ploughed up by 1968; acres of chalk downland in Dorset, once supporting 20 species of grass, 120 flowers and 7 orchids, were being replaced by just one rye-grass strain. Across the nation, artificial rye-grass leys had increased twenty-fold in forty years. They could support not a single butterfly, and 95% of these most attractive insects faced extinction by the end of the century were the trends to be continued.

The destruction was not entirely news to conservation professionals – but nobody had ever pulled the figures together so graphically, related them to real places, and put the blame on agriculture's finance. This Shoard detailed: to start with, machinery could be written off against tax (encouraging over-mechanisation and costing the taxpayer £200m a year); then there were capital grants, for fencing to replace hedges, and other work such as drainage – available to any farmer without regard to his need. Paul Getty would have qualified for a drainage grant at 37–70%, or for moorland ploughing at 22–50%. In 1979/80 those grants cost £171m (as against under £20m spent on countryside conservation). Yet this was dwarfed by the £1,585m cost to taxpayers and consumers, in 1980, of operating the Common Agricultural Policy Price Support system, which encouraged limitless increases in production. Even the farmer's own Ministry (why was it necessary? – we didn't need one for other industries) with 13,600 employees, swallowed £94m. Farmers were also exempted from rates, costing Britain's hard-pressed County Councils a sum of £150m a year, eroding the standard of rural services such as public transport (for those who were not farmers with their own transport) and increasing reliance on the Rate Support Grant paid for by urban taxes. In all, Shoard calculated that supporting agriculture cost the taxpayer and consumer around five billion pounds a year.

Far from being the independent yeoman, each farmer cost the taxpayer more than five times as much as each steel worker in annual subsidies. The Dan Archer image could not stand much of this.

Nor could the fudgers of the conservation world continue to

call confidently for a compromise solution. The 'Shoardite fringe' became a term of abuse both among the NFU–CLA cabals and the old school of conservation. But, with their supporters highly alarmed at the statistics of destruction and the feather-bedding of agriculture, conservation groups said little when Shoard wrote:

> What we have here is a collision of two value systems that are really gearing up to a civil war. . . .

> . . . although few people realise it, the English landscape is under sentence of death. Indeed the sentence is already being carried out. The executioner is not the industrialist or the property speculator, whose activities have touched only the fringes of our countryside. Instead it is the figure traditionally viewed as the custodian of the rural scene – the farmer.

Although consensus conservation worthies, like Derek Barber of the Countryside Commission, made speeches accusing supporters of Marion Shoard's proposed solution – the extension of planning development controls over agriculture and forestry – of wanting to swim through 'rivers of blood' to achieve countryside protection, both the voluntary and official organisations were dragged willy nilly in the direction of demanding stronger controls, when the debate over Shoard's issues spilled over into Parliament.

Paradise Lost

In February 1981, the NCC released data from a comprehensive sampling study of habitat loss which it had begun in May 1980. While it came too late to have much real effect on the structure of the Bill, the figures showed a vastly greater speed and scale of destruction than anyone had suspected before. Instead of just 4% of SSSIs damaged or destroyed a year, the average figure turned out to be 13%. Even in the council rooms of the County Naturalist Trusts, this raised the dust. Letters flooded in to MPs from enraged constituents; breakfast-time and peak evening radio carried daily accounts of destruction in the countryside and of proceedings in Parliament. Habitat conservation had firmly arrived as a political issue.

The aptly named FoE booklet *Paradise Lost* appeared at this time, and gives an account of the losses. However, the full list, as issued to Parliamentarians, is given below.

Habitat Losses in the Counties

ENGLAND

Avon

50% of unimproved meadows in the new county of Avon were destroyed in the ten years up to 1980.

Bedfordshire and Huntingdon

In Bedfordshire 70% loss in wetlands in 25 years; 14 SSSIs (28%) destroyed or damaged since 1951.

In Huntingdon 88% of hedgerows lost in 30 years.

Berkshire, Buckinghamshire and Oxfordshire

A re-survey of 61 of the 249 flood-plain meadows in Oxfordshire identified in 1978 has shown that 12 (20%) have been lost, mainly ploughed up.

Cambridgeshire

17% of woodland lost in 35 years.

Cheshire

7% of SSSIs seriously damaged in 1980.

Cornwall

In the 13 years to 1976 more hedges were lost than in the previous 75 years.

Cumbria

This county has nearly half the total number of limestone pavement sites in Britain. Nationally, a survey revealed that only 3% of pavements are 100% intact, mainly because of stone removed for horticultural use.

Devon

In the 20 years up to 1972, 20% of Devon's woodlands were destroyed. 67% of rough grassland and heath (outside National Parks) lost this century.

Dorset

In south-east Dorset 38% of important botanical sites have been partly or totally changed in the last 50 years.

Three-quarters of southern heathland lost in the last 50 years. 32% SSSIs seriously damaged during 1980.

Durham

A survey of 11 sites known to have suffered damage on or after 1957 showed a reduction in the area of wildlife interest from 3,334 acres to 637 acres (reduction of 80%) rendering the sites unviable.

Essex

9% of SSSIs seriously damaged in 1980.

Hampshire and Isle of Wight

20% of chalk grassland lost since 1966; 19.4% of heathland destroyed in 14 years.

On the Isle of Wight 17.5% of chalk grassland damaged or destroyed in 14 years since 1966.

Hertfordshire and Middlesex

In Herts 56% of ancient woods destroyed since 1850; 99.5% mossland destroyed or damaged by 1978.

Kent

40% SSSIs designated since 1951 have now been damaged or destroyed.

Lancashire

99.5% of the lowland bogs have been reclaimed.

Lincolnshire

At least 50% of ancient grassland lost in the last 30 years.

Norfolk

Only three Broads remain substantially unpolluted and one of the three is currently under threat from enrichment from a pump drainage scheme.

Northamptonshire

20% partial or complete habitat loss since 1960 (9 of 44 sites), 54% of sites having some loss (24 of 44 sites). Of 30 proposed SSSIs, 10 are under immediate threat.

Northumberland

33% loss or damage of SSSIs in last 15 years.

Nottinghamshire

90% of ponds in East Nottinghamshire have been lost in the last 25 years.

Shropshire

600 prime sites for wildlife identified in county survey; 19 lost in last 18 months.

Somerset

Street Heath SSSI (Grade I NCR) – on January 14, 1981, planning permission given for peat winning.

Staffordshire

25% of SSSIs damaged in last 10 years.

Suffolk

70% of Breckland Heath lost (part in Norfolk).

Sussex

25% loss or damage in last 15 years.

Wiltshire

29 out of 50 downland SSSIs have suffered some loss of scientific interest in recent years as a direct result of agriculture.

Worcestershire

35% loss of ponds in 55 years to 1971; 17% of SSSIs damaged in last 25 years.

Yorkshire

Wakefield Metropolitan District has lost 23.39% of woodland cover in 17 years to 1978, almost entirely to agriculture.

WALES

Powys

7% of moorland destroyed in six years.

SCOTLAND

Dumfries and Galloway

90% of heathland lost.

An Act of Self-interest

Actions, as the proverb observes, speak louder than words. So despite winning the press debate almost hands down, it came as little surprise when the conservation lobby failed to make much impact on the *Wildlife and Countryside Bill*, which emerged as an Act very much in line with the wishes of the National Farmers Union and the Country Landowners Association. Environmentalists were up against a political and propaganda machine which has been described by at least one ex-Minister as 'the most powerful lobby in Britain, probably in Europe', and was credited, as long ago as 1962, with having a relationship with government 'unique in its range and intensity'. So effective is the NFU lobbying machine that it was used as a model by the Confederation of British Industry when it wished to increase its influence over Labour MPs.

Graham Cox and Philip Lowe recall that, during the passage of the Bill:

> . . . the NFU's lobbying was by far the most extensive and detailed of any of the groups involved. In all, it issued 13 parliamentary briefing papers. The average list of recipients in the Lords was 150, whereas in the Commons the 'short agricultural list' is 70 and the 'long list' 350. These lists were computerised, carefully amended as necessary, and any MP who showed an interest in something of concern to the NFU could be supplied with additional background material, tapes and interview facilities . . . the NFU with three representatives from the land use division working full-time on the Bill, was the only group with the resources to be present at all stages of the Bill's passage through both houses. . . .

Throughout the Bill's passage, the Government only made concessions to the conservation case where these were forced upon it by guile or by short-term expediency. An example of the former was the inclusion of the otter as a species to be protected in Scotland, achieved at the last moment before the Bill went to Parliament, when FoE confronted Hector Munro (then Minister at the Department of the Environment) with the apparent contradiction of the last remaining otter hunt flourishing in his constituency of Dumfries, and under the guidance of Captain Bell-Irving, Master of the Hunt and former chairman of the Dumfries Conservative Association. On most matters, however, Government remained implacable: a secret Cabinet Committee dominated by landowners William Whitelaw and Francis Pym decided major issues, Pym being said to be 'even more protective of farmers than the NFU'.

The key Part II of the Bill dealing with habitats proved most contentious. The government proposed to protect a small number (around forty) of SSSIs on which owners or occupiers would have to give twelve months' notice to NCC (subject to a fine) of any damaging operations. Actual protection of these would rely on purely voluntary (though financial) agreements between farmers and NCC. Clearly this left out the 3,460 other SSSIs and the rest of the countryside. After publication of the 'Paradise Lost' habitat destruction data in 1981, the Government introduced its own amendment in the Lords, enabling Ministers to issue a voluntary Code of Conduct on SSSIs for all owners and occupiers. Nevertheless, lobbied strongly by the CLA and NFU, it threw out amendments aimed at giving protection to all SSSIs and empowering Ministers to make Porchester-style Moorland Conservation Orders.

The non-agricultural amendments passed in the Lords against Government wishes (marine reserves, 'the Sandford amendment', shooting restrictions, etc.), only survived the Commons stages because, as was noted earlier, the Opposition threatened to talk the Bill out.

As Cox and Lowe say, the Government also:

> . . . made a number of tactical concessions. These included full protection for limestone pavements . . . marine nature reserves . . . and crucially, a requirement that owners of SSSIs give three months' notice of their intention to carry out any potentially damaging operations.

This feeble protection extended to all SSSIs was enough to alarm the NFU and CLA who regarded it as compulsion. On grants in SSSIs, National Parks and on moorland, the Government merely gave MAFF a reminder to consider conservation but only so far as was compatible with the agricultural intent of the scheme. Furthermore, the Government now insisted that if a grant was turned down because the NCC or County Planning Authority (in National Parks) thought it might damage a SSSI or other area, then the NCC or the Planning Authority would have to pay up instead of MAFF. As conservationists pointed out, this turned MAFF grants into a farmer's 'birthright' rather than an incentive to do something on the land for public benefit. Financial Guidelines and the Code of Conduct were published after the Act itself was passed.

Cash or Crisis

A report *Cash or Crisis*, published in 1982 by the British Association of Nature Conservationists and FoE, gives a breakdown of how the Act functions and the difficulties in implementing it fairly, as seen at the time. Perhaps the Act's most striking aspect is how it illuminates the scale, and consequences, of agricultural support. Many of these facts had been hitherto unsuspected or disguised in MAFF's rules of 'confidentiality'.

In general, the Act guaranteed that an owner or occupier would get the money which the Ministry of Agriculture or the Forestry Commission would pay out, and which would involve destroying a site for intensification, even if the destruction was thought to be against the public interest. If protection was agreed, the money would still be paid (on a hypothetical loss-of-profits basis) but the NCC or local authority (in National Parks) would have to find the cash, not the vastly richer MAFF or EEC agricultural purse. As the NCC's annual budget was only £11m and the Government increased it by just £600,000, a crisis was clearly on the cards. Moreover, responsible landowners like the National Trust, or conservation-minded farmers who did not threaten to develop sites, would get nothing. As Malcolm MacEwen said:

> The Act is a hot air balloon, kept aloft by burning public money. The Act rewards the non-conserving farmers, the get-rich-quick merchants, the rural rapists.

In 1982 NCC estimated that implementing the Act would require an extra £2m a year (which the Government did not provide) while RSPB thought it was at least double that, and the *Cash or Crisis* report used the figures from the test-case at Walland Marsh (part of Romney Marsh, Kent) where the NCC had backed off in the face of demands for purchase at £4,000/ha or a three-year drainage moratorium at £400/ha, to show a real likely cost of over £11m for all SSSIs under threat. Halvergate Marshes and other cases soon followed, and it became clear that the Act's implementation might be more controversial than its passage. On a waterlogged Scottish peat bog, Lord Thurso was rewarded with a staggering £278,734 to induce him not to plant conifer trees. On a North Kent farm, the NCC calculated that just one SSSI was going to cost £100,000 a year because the difference was worked out between low-input, low-output grazing marsh, and drained, intensive, profitable acreage. Such payments changed the whole method and rationale of conservation, ransoming the future of wildlife to the profit-motivation of whoever happened to be owner or occupier of the land at the time.

Yet by 1983 conservation groups were afraid that this system, however costly and fundamentally inequitable, was not being applied widely enough, the reason being that NCC was failing to 'renotify' SSSIs at the promised rate. 'Renotification' involves surveying an

SSSI, finding and contacting the owner, registering the SSSI designation as a land charge (i.e. in the deeds), and furnishing her or him with a list of potentially damaging operations. Originally the Government had pledged that renotification would be complete within a year (by the end of 1982), then by 1983, then 'substantially' complete by 1984. At the time of writing, some NCC regions don't expect to complete renotification until 1986, leaving sites outside the Act's protection until then. The failure to renotify sites also removes the possibility of damaged sites appearing as embarrassing statistics of loss, or having to make costly agreements to protect them.

The pump of hot air which, as MacEwen so rightly observed, is now required to keep conservation aloft, is the EEC system of price support, and the British system of forestry finance. Porchester demonstrated that even if all the important land on Exmoor were removed from the system of agricultural intensification, the loss to the nation in food production would be just 0.003% of mutton and 0.0005% of beef. Clearly the nation can afford this, and the agricultural case for developing any other National Park or SSSI is just as weak. The truth is, therefore, that 'compensation' under the Act is handed out simply because farmers and foresters exercise a quite undemocratic influence over government.

The agricultural sums involved are so large because the system of support has reached escape velocity, in terms of both finance and inspired lunacy. It has been lucidly described in Richard Body's book *Agriculture: The Triumph and the Shame*. In 1980/1 the effective level of support for agriculture from the taxpayer and consumer was 166%. This astonishing figure arises because costs of storing and disposing of surpluses must be added to the costs of agricultural intervention which keep prices high for farmers, and tariffs imposed against imports, to keep them out. As a percentage of farmers' income (in practice rates of support for different products vary greatly), taxpayers' support rose to this figure in 1980/1 from around 23% in 1973/4 before Britain joined the EEC, and was forecast to reach 188% in 1981/2. Any reasonable analysis would suggest that as the taxpayer funds a farmer's actions, she or he ought to have a say in what these are. Furthermore, on SSSIs and in National Parks where intensive agriculture is not wanted, we could at least reduce the subsidy to 100%. The current system only encourages expansion of the most profitable agricultural crops (e.g. barley, rape) on to all land. So, for instance, while only 17% of the country is really suitable (Grade I and II) for arable cropping, the proportion had risen to 37% in 1980.

But it would be quite wrong to suggest that this appalling

system benefits all farmers equally; indeed, some suffer greatly from it. Livestock farmers, for example, find it expensive to buy grain feedstuffs. In their study *New Life in the Hills*, Geoffrey Sinclair and Malcolm MacEwan have shown considerable imbalances within hill farming.

The way MAFF handles the EEC's Less Favoured Areas (LFA) Directive monies means that larger farmers who need it least, get most, whereas small farmers get least. The irony is that the Directive aims not to increase production but to ensure continuance of farming, yet MAFF policies have the opposite effect. It is feared that in the Western Isles of Scotland, the IDP (Integrated Development Programme) may prove a similar social blight. To return to the Sinclair–MacEwen study, they show that of the £54.2m LFA funds spent among 20,751 farmers in upland Britain in 1980, the largest 759 farms with 300 or more livestock units (1 unit = 1 cow or 6 sheep) swallowed up 22.4% of the money, giving each large farmer around £13,000 compared with the average of £590 received by the 11,000 smallest farmers with under 50 units. At the same time, bigger farms attract more capital grants for sheds, drainage and so on, and amalgamations proliferate. As a result of such policies, over 5,000 tenant farmers are being bankrupted from the industry each year. The social and ecological costs are inseparable.

In such circumstances it is perhaps no surprise to learn that the NFU, which still effectively dictates MAFF policies, is dominated by large, cereal-producing farmers from SE England. But also, and more encouragingly, some farmers are reacting to these inequities. A *Farmers Weekly* poll in January 1983 showed that while 100% had supported joining the EEC, and 92% had still been in favour in 1975, by 1983 a significant 16% wanted Britain to withdraw. This shift was most marked in the north among small farmers, of whom only 42% felt better off under the EEC. South-east cereal growers, however, remain strong EEC supporters. Furthermore, 78% of all farmers wanted action taken to reduce surpluses, and 48% opposed subsidised sales to countries outside the EEC.

The Berwyns and Forestry

One of the early failures of the *Wildlife and Countryside Act* involved Britain's other major land-use scandal: forestry. The setting was the Berwyn range of mountains, just south of Snowdonia. Here the RSPB had pointed out in 1977 that the area held three of only 13 tracts of upland Wales to have been spared agricultural intensification and afforestation. 148,200 acres (60,000 ha) were of SSSI standard, comprising open heather moor along with wet flushes rich in species like the rare few-flowered sedge, and the Berwyn berry or cloud berry, an amber coloured blackberry collected locally since Roman times. The mountains are also the main area for a number of birds of prey, such as merlin, hen harrier, and peregrine, declining across Europe. NCC's reaction had been to botch a compromise with forestry and agriculture interests.

By 1982, trees were being planted on Llanbrynmair Moors, one of the key botanical areas, 'sacrificed' in a NCC compromise which left habitat for harriers to nest in on one side of the fence, while it covered their feeding grounds with trees on the other. By not designating this and other important areas as SSSI, the NCC avoided triggering the potentially expensive mechanisms of the *Wildlife and Countryside Act*, and avoided conflict with local forestry interests. Eventually it was forced to proceed on some areas, after public threats of court action from the RSPB and FoE (FoE had previously pressed for prosecution over Crymlyn Bog in South Wales and had established that NCC has a duty to notify any site which it knows to be of SSSI standard).

But what incensed conservation groups most was not simply NCC's retreat from its duty, or the doubtful status of its Welsh Committee (this included, for example, D. G. Badham, a member of the Economic Forestry Group, a Director of Economic Forestry Holdings Ltd., Chairman of Economic Forestry Wales Ltd., Chairman of Economic Forestry Holdings Ltd., who listed his *Who's Who* recreation as 'forestry'), but the fact that the forests being planted were not only damaging to wildlife but were unproductive and uneconomic by normal definitions.

Despite its name, the Economic Forestry Group is one of a number of organisations carrying out planting for private clients, not with the object of producing timber but to establish a sound invest-ment. The 'soundness' is based almost wholly on tax advantages. These were investigated by the Parliamentary Committee of Public Accounts in 1980. They found that during planting or replanting when costs are considerable, a syndicate will buy forest areas, and operate them under Tax Schedule D: this allows them to set the net loss against taxable income earned elsewhere (e.g. from property development). Such syndicates then avoid making a profit (and hence losing the tax advantage) by selling up just before the thinning stage, when income accrues. When this happens the plantation reverts automatically to Schedule B. The new owner can then reap profits unhindered from thinnings and fellings, because under Schedule B tax is at a nominal rate, normally on a third of the annual value of the land, irrespective of the actual income. Profits from sale of trees standing or felled are exempt from Capital Gains Tax and are not otherwise taxable. The Public Accounts study estimated that around £10m of tax was lost at 1977 rates through this wonderful racket every year (enough to run the NCC).

On top of this, the Forestry Commission were duty bound to provide grants for planting on the Berwyns, even though officers admitted privately that the area was too windswept to be economic by their own (questionable) standards. Furthermore, the employment value of forestry, which is often dragged in to justify such projects, is not strong. A 1972 Treasury Study revealed that although it was marginally more than that of hill farming, the costs in resources and public money were considerably higher.

Conifer plantations are attractive to a few species – rather like a field of brassicas to a cabbage white butterfly – but utterly hostile to most. The loss of open moor and mountain habitat is obvious, but the coniferisation and conversion of ancient woods to modern plantation is rather less obvious but just as serious.

The NCC estimates that 30–50% of Britain's ancient woodland has been destroyed since 1947, and all the rest will be lost by 2025 except that within nature reserves. For the 250–300,000 ha of ancient forest remnants that remain, the prospects are bleak, as Forestry Commission grant-aid policy is hostile to traditional management. For example, no grants are available for coppicing, which mimics many natural processes and is good for populations of birds, plants and insects. Instead, grants encourage new planting. Licences are required for felling woodland (MAFF grant-aid of 22½% is available for removal of stumps; 50% for drainage of felled areas) but even these do not apply if timber is under a certain diameter (termed 'scrub' by foresters): for example, most coppices. When conifers are planted up throughout a wood, a deep slow-rotting needle layer forms, eliminating even the populations of buried seed from the native flora, so rendering recovery impossible.

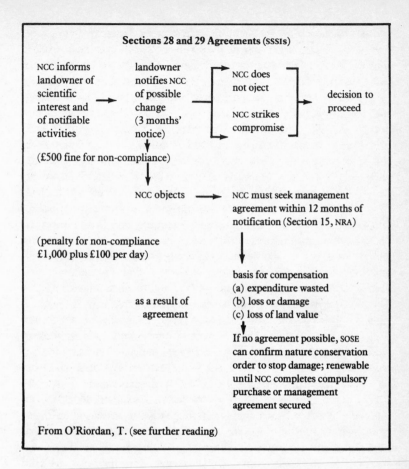

Sections 28 and 29 Agreements (SSSIs)

NCC informs landowner of scientific interest and of notifiable activities → landowner notifies NCC of possible change (3 months' notice)

NCC does not oject

NCC strikes compromise

decision to proceed

(£500 fine for non-compliance)

NCC objects → NCC must seek management agreement within 12 months of notification (Section 15, NRA)

(penalty for non-compliance £1,000 plus £100 per day)

as a result of agreement

basis for compensation
(a) expenditure wasted
(b) loss or damage
(c) loss of land value

If no agreement possible, SOSE can confirm nature conservation order to stop damage; renewable until NCC completes compulsory purchase or management agreement secured

From O'Riordan, T. (see further reading)

Conclusions

The activities of Internal Drainage Boards, Water Authorities, and the threats from acid rain, nitrate build-up in water supply, power station construction and oil pollution, all merit the detailed discussion given to agriculture above. But space and priorities preclude that.

However overwhelming the odds stacked against wildlife in the countryside may seem to be, there are signs of hope and glimmers of light in even the least expected quarters. Poor Sir Ralph Verney got himself burned in effigy by farmers on the Somerset Levels, when he tried to get them to accept SSSI designation in spring 1983. Being burned did little to save the Levels, as the NCC Region stood meekly by as drainage ploughed ahead, but it salvaged something of Sir Ralph's reputation in conservation circles. He was sacked soon after by the Secretary of State for the Environment, Tom King, himself a local MP and farmer.

At the time of writing the conservation movement is pondering how to implement the 'UK Response to the World Conservation Strategy', a pompous document of over 500 pages, which was produced in response to a clarion call to solve today's problems tomorrow but which looks more like a recipe for procrastination *ad infinitum*. Yet its basic message of conservation-with-development is not all bad, especially if it means conservation-as-development. The farmers of West Sedgemoor, for example, might not view wildlife conservation as so inhibiting, if their object in land management was conservation farming presented as every bit as technically challenging as the odd concept of cramming ever greater concentrations of growth-inducing chemicals into the soil, then dousing them in rising amounts of chemicals to kill off the life that is encouraged, only to produce excess amounts of excessively expensive protein, carbohydrate and fat.

There is no doubt that the present philosophies of agricultural and forestry policy are totally bankrupt. The alternatives are also quite well known, and technically feasible. But to exercise the necessary common sense and secure political change, environmentalists must organise and assert their political strength. We do have the right to say how our heritage of resources is used and conserved. One of the most hopeful, spontaneously supported developments in conservation over the last decade has been the blossoming of 'urban conservation' groups, city nature parks and ecological gardens. If this spirit of participative ecological democracy can be transferred to the countryside, then there will be a future for our ancient woodlands, meadows and hedgerows once more.

Further Reading

Body, R. 1982, *Agriculture: The Triumph and the Shame*, Temple-Smith, London.

Chapman, P. 1975, *Fuel's Paradise*, Penguin, London.

Cox, G. and Lowe, P. 1983, 'The Battle Not The War: The Politics of the Wildlife and Countryside Act' in *Countryside Planning Yearbook* Vol. 4, pp. 48–76.

ECOS: A Review of Conservation journal (quarterly) published by the British Association of Nature Conservationists. Covers countryside and wildlife issues in depth. Contact: BANC membership secretary, Rectory Farm, Stanton St. John, Oxfordshire.

FoE (King, A. and Conroy, C.) 1981, *Paradise Lost*, Friends of the Earth, London (377 City Road, EC1, 01 837 0731).

Green, B. 1981, *Countryside Conservation* , Allen and Unwin, London.

Lowe, P. and Goyder, J. 1983, *Environmental Groups in Politics*, Allen and Unwin, London.

Mabey, R. 1980, *The Flowering of Britain*, Hutchinson, London.

Mabey, R. 1983, *The Common Ground: A Place for Nature in Britain's Future*, Hutchinson, London.

MacEwen, Anne and Malcolm, 1982, *National Parks: Conservation and Cosmetics*, Allen and Unwin, London.

North, R. 1983, *Wild Britain: The Century Book of Marshes, Fens and Broads*, Century, London.

O'Riordan, T. 1983, 'Rural: Putting Trust in the Countryside' in *The Conservation and Development Programme for the UK; A Response to the World Conservation Strategy*, Kogan Page, London.

Shoard, M. 1980, *The Theft of the Countryside*, Maurice Temple-Smith, London.

Sinclair, G. and MacEwen, M. 1983, *New Life for the Hills*, Council for National Parks, 3 Hobart Place, London, SW1.

Warren, A. and Goldsmith, F. B. (Eds) 1983, *Conservation In Perspective*, Wiley, Chichester.

DAVID BALDOCK
4 Land Use: A test of priorities

LAND USE IS NOT a term which immediately ignites passion; it is rather dry and unprepossessing, the parlance of planners and academics. Yet it has been at the centre of many of the battles in which the environmental movement has engaged over the last 15 years. It has been schemes to mine copper in Snowdonia, drain wetlands, build motorways, find sites for nuclear waste dumping and construct airports which have focused campaigns and started national debates. Nor is interest limited to individual sites; there is great and growing concern about the loss of wildlife habitat, the expansion of forestry, and the role of the planning system.

With 55 million people packed into a relatively small area, conflict over land use is inescapable and thousands of proposals are under discussion or in dispute at any one time. Some are of purely local consequence, such as the designation of a new footpath, but others have almost infinite ramifications. After an unparalleled Odyssey of investigation and inquiry on the subject of a third London Airport, fundamental points have yet to be settled and new proposals continue to emerge.

Almost all land-use questions have an environmental dimension and conversely most environmental questions have a land-use aspect.

The CEGB's wish to build a PWR at Sizewell is being opposed not solely on technical and economic grounds, but also because the site chosen is in a beautiful part of the Suffolk Heritage Coast.

Land use is a common thread through many issues of environmental importance, from waste disposal to mineral extraction, from forestry to transport planning. The common aims are to reject inappropriate forms of development, find a satisfactory balance between competing uses and generally to conserve and enhance natural resources, protecting the land itself from pollution, degradation, and destruction.

The Passing of Wilderness

Before man emerged as a significant influence on the scene, the 'natural' land use of the British Isles was the climax vegetation. Britain was largely covered in forest, the vast majority of it broad-leaved, with a limited area of pine in Scotland. The variety of indigenous tree species was small and the landscape was dominated by familiar trees such as oak, ash, birch and willow. Alongside the forest were areas of marsh and fen, covering substantial tracts of land, especially around river estuaries like the Wash. Forests reached up the hills to at least 2,000 feet, then gave way to shrub, composed mostly of juniper and willow, and at higher levels still to low alpines, grass and lichens. Wetlands were also common in the hills, comprising wet moorlands and bog.

The eradication of this natural vegetation by man has been surprisingly complete. The areas that survive, such as patches of Caledonian pine forest, are no more than remnants. Even in the wilder parts of the uplands, most habitats have been greatly altered by human activity, especially deforestation. For many centuries the regular burning of moorland and the widespread introduction of grazing animals has been active in removing the cover, draining wetlands, converting the better land for cultivation or livestock rearing and establishing human settlements of an increasingly extensive kind. In the last two centuries the process has accelerated rapidly – the area of heathland in Dorset today is only about 15% of what it was in 1760. The area of lowland bog in northern England and Scotland has also fallen to 15% of its former size, but in one century rather than two. In the last 30 years there has been a particularly intense onslaught on the areas remaining. Although now recognised as an important habitat for rare species such as the

Dartford warbler and sand lizard, the area of Dorset heathland has been cut in half since 1962.

This process has resulted in three dominant forms of land use: agriculture, forestry and urban development. Agriculture has much the largest share of the UK's 24 million hectares, absorbing about 19 million ha, or approximately 79% of the total. Woodland of all kinds is now confined to about 9% of the land area and the remaining 12% is predominantly in urban use. The urban land comprises not only towns and villages, but also roads, highways, reservoirs, mines and other forms of development in the countryside. These peripheral developments can be particularly demanding in their land requirements; even in 1962 there were an estimated 66,500 ha of roadside verges in England and Wales according to Sir Dudley Stamp. Motorways claimed another 12,000 ha between 1968 and 1978.

Outside the offshore islands and parts of northern Scotland little true wilderness now remains, and very small areas of Britain are devoted solely to conservation. With farmland worth around £2,000 per acre, areas set aside for wildlife seem an expensive luxury to many landowners. Nor has the state chosen to intervene on behalf of the wilderness. National Parks are not publicly owned unlike in the United States for example – and even nature reserves are rarely owned by the community. The NCC only owns about 14% by area of the key sites designated as National Nature Reserves, although they cover no more than a modest 136,000 ha. The 4,000 Sites of Special Scientific Interest, which cover an area ten times this size, are mostly used for agriculture or forestry and receive very limited protection.

Of course, nature protection does not depend on the outright ownership of land and it is only in recent decades that the conflicts between farming and forestry on the one hand and wildlife on the other have become so sharp (see Chapter 3). Multiple land use with several different objectives being pushed within one area is often a desirable goal, particularly in Britain where the total surface available is so limited. However, recent developments have made it increasingly elusive in practice. The new farmed landscape, divided into large fields bordered by barbed wire fences, increasingly denuded of old spinneys and hedges and populated with quasi-industrial buildings, can be as inhospitable for ramblers, picnickers and wildfowlers as it is for wildlife. The countryside is sometimes described as the farmer's falling star and all too often the farmer expects extensive use of it.

Traditional methods of farm and forest management involved a close integration of arable and stock farming, of fuel and timber production, of recreation, sport and agriculture, of wildlife habitat and economic activity. Now, however, the countryside is used more intensively, and for increasingly specialised purposes. The needs of different activities are more sharply defined and more often in conflict. Multiple land use has become a conscious goal, to be achieved by effort and compromise, and sometimes legal intervention.

Ownership and Control

In urban areas, where there is an active land market, it is rare for individuals to own more than a small area and the planning system, despite its imperfections, provides a means of curbing inappropriate development and zoning land for particular uses. Land use is subject to some democratic as well as economic pressures. Planning committees are made up of elected representatives and there is some provision for public participation. Perhaps most usefully, people have the opportunity to object to proposed developments in their immediate neighbourhood. The merits of this system should not be exaggerated. Participation is often limited and most exploited by the articulate and affluent. Nevertheless, the community has some sort of say in the way the land is disposed of.

In the countryside, land is owned by fewer people, changes hands less often, and is infrequently available for rent. Democratic control over land use is weaker and agricultural and forestry operations almost entirely escape the provisions of the Town and Country Planning Acts. There can be dramatic changes in land-use without any opportunity for public intervention. Forests can be planted or felled; marshes drained and converted to arable production, large new buildings erected, rivers canalised and landscape features like hedgerows removed altogether. Not only does this affect wildlife, it can have a considerable impact on the lives of individuals, for example, people who find themselves living next to intensive pig units. In the past, change took place much more gradually and although few people owned land, rural life revolved around agriculture; there was an intimate relationship between villages and the land that surrounded them. This is no longer so.

A century ago, 80% of Britain was owned by perhaps as few as 7,000 landowners. Today, it is estimated that 1,500 individuals may still own about a third of England and Wales and a further 100 probably own about a quarter of Scotland. Other large tracts are owned by institutions, both old and new. For centuries, the Crown, the Church, and Oxbridge colleges have owned extensive areas, often keeping direct control of woodland and dividing the remainder into tenant farms. In recent years they have been joined by a new set of institutions, particularly property and insurance companies, and pension funds.

We do not know exactly how much land these new commercial institutions have acquired because reliable figures are not collected but they are a powerful force in the market, buying up around 20,000 ha annually.

Unencumbered by capital transfer tax, the new institutions are particularly concerned with the long-term investment value of land and they concentrate on buying the best, especially good quality land in the eastern half of Britain. In this part of the country, farms are already of above average size and above average value. Predominantly arable and usually heavily mechanised, these farms have become valuable businesses beyond the reach of all but a tiny handful of individuals. A good 1,000 acre farm in Lincolnshire (408 ha), by no means an enormous holding, is likely to be worth around £3 million. In areas like this the yeoman farmer is likely to become as obsolete as the horse.

Another threatened species is the tenant farmer. The new institutional owners tend to install professional farm managers to run their estates for them, rather than create a tenancy which will give a family security for three generations. Private landlords and other institutions are now increasingly reluctant to create new tenancies, preferring to take land 'in hand', usually under a manager, both for tax reasons and to increase their control. Tenant farms, like privately rented accommodation in cities, have gone into decline, owner occupancy rising from about 54% of farms in 1960/61 to around 66% today – a remarkable increase given that only about 1% of agricultural land comes on to the market in any one year.

The high price of land and the extreme shortage of tenancies make it difficult for people born outside agriculture to enter the profession unless they have access to large sums of money. Agricultural workers, whose numbers are also dwindling rapidly, have little chance of ever acquiring their own holdings, especially since the Land Settlement Association has been wound up. The position has been made even worse by the Government's recent squeeze on local authority spending. This has forced many County Councils to look around for disposable assets. Many have decided to sell at least some of their small holdings, traditionally regarded as the bottom rung of the farming ladder. County Council small holdings have been one of the last sources of small let farms and market gardens and although their value to new entrants and young farmers was often exaggerated, their sale further reduces access to farm land. Feelings on the issue have run high and even the NFU have been reported as describing Somerset's plan to sell off its 250 holdings as 'bare-faced asset stripping'.

While small holdings and tenancies disappear the total number of farms continues to fall. About 2,000 farms cease to exist every year, with the smallest holdings most affected. There is a relentless trend towards amalgamation, buying bigger fields, bigger buildings, and continued readjustment of the landscape. When a farmer retires or sells his holding it may either be disposed of as one unit or increasingly often separated into lots and sold to neighbouring farms. This is one of the most important ways in which farms continue to get larger. 'Lotting' pushes up local prices and makes sales easier. In a recent MAFF survey of farm sales in the West Midlands, 60% of the land sold in the period 1977–80 was divided into lots, fetching prices £400 an acre higher than for unlotted land. The average size of the farm in the area rose from 162 acres to 182 acres and only a fifth of the farms sold remained as full-time units. This method of sale tended to create a number of small part-time units on land surrounding old farmhouses often bought by affluent newcomers and also resulted in 10% of the land sold being lost to agriculture altogether.

There remain about 245,000 farms in Britain, roughly half of which are part-time, particularly common in Northern Ireland and Wales. Part-time farms between them probably occupy no more than 10% of the total agricultural area. Indeed, over 80% of Britain's agricultural land is divided into about 80,000 large farms, which are steadily increasing in size. The average size of a full-time farm is now around 120 ha, a bit less than 300 acres, and it is the decisions made on these relatively large units which determine the shape of the countryside. Mechanisation has proceeded even faster than amalgamation and the size and shape of fields and buildings is increasingly tailored to the requirements of an expanding galaxy of machines. The monumental scale of many new barns, silos and slurry stores, and the growing neglect of dry stone walls and other time-absorbing landscape features are some of the most visible signs of the disappearing work force. 540,000 full-time workers in 1949 have dwindled to around 175,000 today.

Britain's large farms and small agricultural payroll are regarded with considerable enthusiasm at MAFF which considers that this relatively modern farm structure gives us an important competitive advantage over other EEC countries with a much larger agricultural population. In an era in which economies of scale have become almost axiomatic, this seems only common sense. In reality, however, the relationship between size and efficiency is far from clear, and research does not suggest that the largest holdings are any more productive than medium-sized farms employing one to two people. Bigger farms have not brought benefits to wildlife either. The new larger units are more heavily capitalised and the acquisition of land at high prices has increased agriculture's burden of indebtedness. The resulting pressure to earn adequate returns has added to the attractions of intensive management and the elimination of unproductive earners. Many traditional skills have been lost as the workforce dwindles and few newcomers can afford to experiment with ecologically sensitive management.

The accumulation of land into fewer hands has generated a growing unease inside and outside the farming world. With tenants and small farms disappearing, the ownership of land is becoming increasingly remote from local communities. Villages can no longer depend on agriculture for employment and many are now undergoing dramatic social change, facing either depopulation or the displacement of people working on the land by commuters, service sector workers and the elderly. New organisations, such as the Small Farmers' Association, the Tenant Farmers' Association and the Farmers' Union of Wales, have sprung up to defend the interests of groups which are in danger of being swept off the land. The Tenant Farmers' Association recently suggested that there should be strong discouragement of farms of more than 2,000 acres. This sounds a timid step, especially alongside the tough controls of farm size operating in Denmark and parts of France, but it is a radical proposal for a British farming organisation. Without measures of this kind, it is clear that farms will continue to grow larger and more like the giant holdings common in the United States. If this happens, villages will become almost wholly severed from their past: pleasant residential communities, largely irrelevant to the needs of agribusiness.

The trend towards large farms and remote ownership is closely paralleled in forestry. The Forestry Commission owns more than 40% of all woodland in Great Britain, and DANI (The Department of Agriculture for Northern Ireland) owns about three-quarters of all woodland in Northern Ireland. The rest is divided between large private forestry, and farmers, who own most of the small woods which survive in the lowlands.

Private investors in forestry frequently delegate the management of their estates to specialised companies. One of the largest of these, the Economic Forestry Group, was responsible for more than 20% of all private sector planting in 1980/81. Both the Forestry Commission and private investors have a preference for large plantations, almost always consisting of conifers – most commonly sitka spruce. New afforestation is concentrated on poor soils in the uplands, especially in Scotland, and over half the current forest area has been planted in the last forty years. For most of this period afforestation has been distinctly unattractive as a commercial proposition and it is usually only worthwhile for private owners because of the favourable tax arrangements for high income earners which were described in Chapter 3. New planting also attracts giants from the Forestry Commission which acts as Forest Authority as well as forest owner and thereby has a commanding influence over the fate of British woodlands. As in agriculture, mechanisation has advanced rapidly in recent years and employment in forestry is now around 20,000 and falling despite an expanding acreage.

The drive to increase output and maximise returns has brought about an increasingly specialised use of land. There are fewer mixed farms or mixed woods, and more specialised pig units and sitka spruce monocultures. Even where the type of farming remains unchanged there can be marked alterations in land use. A growing number of dairy farmers are switching their herds to 'zero grazing', a system whereby cattle and pasture are separated in order to get the maximum returns from each. The cows are confined to a small area, often indoors, and the fields are managed intensively to produce silage or hay, which is fed to them in controlled quantities, thus eliminating the somewhat haphazard process of animals grazing at will.

For pigs and poultry the move indoors is already well established and few changes in the countryside have been as spectacular as the growth of specialised factory farms, some producing none of their own feed. Intensive livestock farms are now spread throughout the country, but like conventional factories they are best located near to markets and with ready access to raw materials – in this case grain. North Humberside now has one of the densest pig populations in Europe and special planning arrangements have been devised accordingly. Arable farms, too, have engaged in a formidable process of intensification – in the last twenty years wheat production has almost quadrupled and barley production doubled. Steady prices, boosted considerably by the Common Agricultural Policy, have made cereal growing consistently profitable and encouraged farmers not only to increase their yields, but to convert as much land as possible to arable production. The area under wheat, barley and oats increased by a third between 1961/62 and 1982/83, at the expense not only of pasture and other agricultural land, but of wetlands and woodlands too. Conversion is still continuing, even though Britain is now a net exporter of all three major cereals. For wetlands particularly the high price of cereals under the CAP has been disastrous, providing landowners with large capital gains from the conversion of grazing marsh to wheat.

Rural land is itself an expensive commodity, rapidly becoming as inaccessible to its traditional occupants as thatched cottages have become for farm workers. Inevitably this widens the gulf between modern farming and forestry businesses and the local communities from which they were once inseparable. However, farmers are often reluctant to recognise the implications of revolutionary change in their own industry. Many resent the recent calls for planning controls without acknowledging that it was the advent of modern farming practices which precipitated this intrusion. Within little more than a generation the landscape has been abruptly rearranged in many parts of Britain and village life transformed. The appeal of planning controls is that they may help to conserve valued parts of the countryside and at the same time offer local communities a new opportunity to influence their surroundings.

Shrinking Acres: Urban Needs Versus Rural Resources

When the first Town and Country Planning Act appeared in 1932 one of the problems which it was designed to address was the urban sprawl which had appeared like a lush new growth in the 1920s and early 1930s. New suburban housing, industry and a rash of accompanying facilities had made deep incursions into the country- side, especially along main roads. These developments were often unsightly, and transformed many rural areas into linear dormitories, but they were also an extravagant use of land, sterilising much larger areas than were actually used. The planning system has evolved considerably since 1932 but the attempt to guide and restrict new development on rural land has continued to be an important objective. This has not been without success; there is little doubt that planning control has prevented the wholesale invasion of the countryside, allowed the establishment of Green Belts, prevented a number of neighbouring communities from merging completely and directed many developments on to appropriate sites. However, the continued loss of large tracts of agricultural land, not to mention woodland, salt marsh and other habitats, remains a cause of concern, particularly since the Government seems committed to easing the restraints on the development of green field sites.

In 1976 the Centre for Agricultural Strategy published a report *Land for Agriculture* in which they took the view that:

> The existing planning process has not been effective in containing urban sprawl and has allowed unnecessary encroachment on agricultural land.

Alice Coleman, writing at around the same time, was even more damning of the planning system, pointing to the growth of idle and underused land in the urban fringe and coining the phrase SLOAP, Space Left Over After Planning. Her second Land Utilisation Survey suggested that there were nearly 110,000 ha of undeveloped but largely unproductive land in and around the urban areas of England and Wales. While it is generally acknowledged that urban land-take has fallen considerably since the 1920s, there is still concern that agriculture can ill afford to continue surrendering large tracts every year. Furthermore, Government attitudes to the role of planning seem to have altered considerably in recent years and there has been an increased emphasis on quick results, the encouragement of new investment and relaxed controls, not least in Green Belts. This new approach was particularly clearly summarised in an important Department of the Environment circular, number 22/80, which asked planning authorities to assist economic legislation by easing restrictions on development. This was introduced by the Minister for Local Government with the words:

> I regard this circular as a most important advance in the evolution of the British planning system. Hitherto, there has been too much emphasis on restraint and restriction. From now on, we intend to ensure that positive attitudes prevail.

This kind of initiative was not what the Centre for Agricultural Strategy had in mind four years earlier when they had argued:

> It is no exaggeration to say that, without a more positive approach to land use planning now, there is a danger of land scarcity in the near future.

Some transfer of farm land to urban uses is unavoidable and indeed essential for the improvement of living and working conditions in cities. Even with a stable population there is a need for new housing, industrial sites, schools, hospitals, recreational facilities and transport systems. Towns and villages in some parts of the country will inevitably attract a growing population while others will decline, particularly when employment opportunities are so unevenly distributed. It must also be acknowledged that despite the predations of urban developers, which may have amounted to as much as 40,000 ha in some years, there is no immediate danger of running out of food. Agricultural output has risen substantially since the war, even on a shrinking acreage. Furthermore, the force of the technical revolution is still not spent – production has risen by about 30% since the end of the 1960s. Although we are only 75% self-sufficient in home-produced temperate foods, this is not necessarily an argument for encouraging farmers to produce more or for giving agriculture priority over other land uses. Surpluses of temperate products have reached crisis level in the EEC, giving rise to wasteful disposal methods and mountainous expenditure. While Britain remains a member of the Community it is impossible to dissociate ourselves from this problem; controls on production are urgently needed and British farmers will not be exempted from them.

The need to protect land from irreversible urban development arises not so much from the immediate requirements of agriculture as from the almost irreplacable value of the resource. Agriculture has been successfully squeezed into a smaller area, but it has only been possible to produce 2–3% more per hectare per year, by a process of rapid intensification. This has depended on an unprecedented rate of technical advance, ample subsidies from the state, and greatly increased use of fertilizers, agrochemicals and fuel. Such favourable conditions are unlikely to be maintained indefinitely – it is already difficult to satisfy the CAP's alarming appetite for funds. Furthermore, intensification has been achieved at considerable cost to the environment and there are now real uncertainties about the sustainability of modern methods.

The long-term effects of heavy fertilizer use on soil fertility are highly uncertain but it is already clear that excessive nitrate levels in the ground water of parts of East Anglia, for example, are attributable to current farming practice. Similarly, it seems unlikely that pests and diseases can be controlled indefinitely by increasingly elaborate chemical cocktails and little is known about the eventual accumulative effect of these substances either on the environment or on human health. We cannot be sure that the key technologies of modern agriculture will continue to be either usable or acceptable. Alternatives may need more land, as indeed does organic agriculture, which rejects the use of fertilizers and pesticides and is free of their accompanying hazards.

There are other reasons too why we may wish to return to more extensive farming systems, perhaps accepting lower yields as the price. The cost of agrochemicals may become prohibitively high, imported inputs like phosphates may become difficult to obtain, factory farming systems may be rejected on animal welfare grounds, and an eventual accommodation between wildlife and modern farming may require some return to more traditional methods. Equally, it may be necessary to produce larger quantities of food in the future, possibly to feed a larger, more affluent population or to increase self-sufficiency levels. It would be foolish to limit any of these options by the unnecesssary transfer of land to urban uses. It is difficult to forecast Britain's future land requirements at all accurately, but it is obvious that continual development confines all rural land uses to a progressively smaller area and leaves a shrinking lake to be divided between farming, forestry, energy production, water supplies, wildlife, sport and recreation. While the development of farm land on the urban fringe in no way justifies the ploughing of moorland, drainage of wetland, felling of ancient woodland and other habitat losses, it is sometimes seen to do so, especially by farmers. On both these frontiers of agriculture the dangers of misallocation of land use are at their greatest, partly because of the large capital sums at stake. Since the expansion of agriculture and forestry into marginal and 'unproductive' land is still subject to little restraint, it is particularly important that the planning system is used effectively to regulate the development of green field sites.

It is difficult to discover how much land is developed every year, especially since the Ministry of Agriculture's figures contain a large element of mysterious 'other adjustments', but it is probably around 20,000 ha, if activities such as mineral extraction are included. There are substantial areas of land for which planning authorities have already consented to development which has yet to take place and there could be a major surge of new applications if the recession ended or the Government released more funds for housing or industrial development. Even during the recent era of declining industrial development and drastically reduced housebuilding, a large volume of new developments have been given permission and private builders are now confident enough to propose 12 new 'villages', of around 20,000 people each, to be built on virgin sites near London, some in the Green Belt.

Local planning authorities are obliged to consult with MAFF

whenever dealing with planning applications which involve the development of significant amounts of agricultural land which are not already ear-marked for development. The Council for the Protection of Rural England have examined the results of this process and argue that the Government is intentionally weakening this safeguard. They show that in England and Wales applications for new development outside previously approved plans have been running at the rate of almost 15,000 ha a year since 1977, and that only 20–25 per cent have been opposed by MAFF. In the first nine months of 1982 fewer than 19% of these applications were opposed.

There is little doubt about the need for new housing. Around 1.1 million dwellings were classified as 'unfit' in the most recent English House Condition Survey and millions more needed very substantial repairs or improvement. People born in the last baby boom of the early 1960s are now entering the housing market and there is a tendency for smaller households including a growing number of people living alone. Continued migration away from inner cities and areas of unemployment to centres of growth, like the Thames Valley and parts of East Anglia, adds to these other pressures.

For industry, too, the attractions of the inner city have waned. Many traditional manufacturing industries are either in decline or on the brink of extinction. Plants are closing and firms are concentrating on fewer sites, often those on the urban fringe. In transport terms, it is usually cheaper to be located near to a motorway than in a city centre; this is particularly important for the distribution and 'Sunrise' industries, such as microelectronics, which are amongst the major consumers of green field sites. A revelation common to many commercial property surveys is that 'Sun-rise' executives feel happier near an airport. Areas such as the Thames Valley are highly attractive to new industries since there is a plentiful supply of skilled labour, transport is convenient, there is a wide variety of amenities, and rent and rates are lower than in inner London.

The temptation to allow urban development to concentrate increasingly on green field sites in thus enormous, especially for local authorities which are trying to create new employment, are short of finance and are under continual siege by developers. Where new motorways or main roads have been built the pressure for development is almost irresistible. Nonetheless, the sacrifice of further areas of rural land is a very costly way of trying to promote growth, even if it is effective, which is by no means certain. This is not solely because of the loss to agriculture and other users of the countryside. Most low density developments on the urban periphery are built for car owners. Distances are often too great for walking and it is difficult to provide an economic public transport service. Built around the road network in the first place, these new settlements and workplaces necessitate its further expansion and add to traffic flows. As schools, hospitals, sports centres and other facilities follow the population to green field sites, they become increasingly inaccessible by public transport and cars are seen as yet more indispensable by those who can afford them. Greater car mileage in turn leads to the familiar symptoms of falling public transport revenues, reduced services, additional congestion and noise, increasing energy consumption, further pollution and more accidents. Low density development is inefficient in energy terms, not least because it requires people to travel greater distances in order to reach employment, education and friends.

By any definition the car is an extravagant consumer of land. Not only is land required for roads, parking areas, garages and a plethora of other services, but further areas must be set aside in Britain and elsewhere to provide an adequate supply of aggregates, raw materials, and fossil fuels to keep the system functioning. While it is functioning, it sprays out lead, at the expense of both human health and urban gardens, and, by adding large quantities of nitrogen oxides to the atmosphere, it almost certainly contributes to the formation of acid rain, affecting soil health and vegetation over very extensive areas.

The costs of concentrating new development outside existing urban areas are not purely environmental. Resources and effort are diverted away from the communities which most need them – the declining inner cities and the dozens of towns built around manufacturing industries which can no longer employ more than a fraction of their traditional workforce. In some of these towns, like Shotton and Corby, almost the entire manufacturing base has been swept away and development here must be a much greater priority than on agricultural land in Berkshire. Government housing and expenditure policy have produced a precipitous fall in local authority housebuilding programmes and although the rehabilitation of older properties is theoretically a keystone of the current approach, the programme has been too small to make a major impact on the enormous backlog of deteriorating dwellings, and local authorities have been massively underspending their financial allocations for the Housing Investment Programme. The consequence is a lack of improved housing in inner urban areas, especially for single people, and correspondingly greater pressure elsewhere.

None of this suggests that it would be useful to try to throttle all growth on green field sites. What is needed is a concentrated effort to revive inner city areas and decaying manufacturing towns – however immense the difficulties. The Government has laid great stress on harnessing private enterprise and voluntary effort for this task – a solution which has the attraction of costing the Exchequer relatively little, but which is quite inadequate for the scale of the problem. To make a real impact it will be necessary to make a more substantial commitment, including the release of significant sums of public money for housing, services, industry and the environment, a serious attack on the problem of unused but prohibitively expensive urban land and the implementation of a more effective policy for channelling investment into urban industry. In most cases land availability would not be a serious constraint.

Most metropolitan areas contain substantial amounts of vacant and derelict land, perhaps 6 or 7% of the total in the older inner cities. In the area covered by the Merseyside Structure Plan alone there are at least 12 square miles of vacant land and a further seven square miles which are likely to become derelict in time. Many of these areas are potentially important sites for new development, but they could also be exploited in dozens of other ways, particularly if they could be made available at a low cost, even on a temporary basis. Friends of the Earth have campaigned actively for new allotments and for urban nature reserves, but there are many other potential uses such as city farms, tree nurseries, adventure play-grounds and so forth. Better use of vacant and derelict land is only a small part of urban renewal, but one in which there is a rare opportunity for direct community involvement.

Forestry

The afforestation of the uplands is proceeding at much the same rate as urbanisation elsewhere, about 20,000 ha a year, mostly in Scotland. This is somewhat slower than in the recent past (twice as much land was being planted in the early 1970s) but it still represents a very substantial change in land use. It also seems to have the blessing of the Government, which would like to see Britain increase its self-sufficiency in timber and believes that:

> A continuing expansion of forestry is in the national interest, both to reduce our dependence upon imported wood in the long-term and to provide continued employment in forestry

and associated industries. There should be scope for new planning to continue in the immediate future broadly at the rate of the past 25 years while preserving an acceptable balance with agriculture, the environment and other interests.

The notion that afforestation is in the national interest is an impressively widespread one. Britain produces only a small fraction of its timber requirements, about 8%, and the general concept of replenishing our diminished woodlands has an immediate appeal. When the Forestry Commission was established immediately after the First World War there was much less forest in the UK than there is now and the Government's objective in building up commercial timber production was primarily strategic. Now the argument is predominantly economic and both the Forestry Commission and its supporters claim that afforestation will prove worthwhile because imported timber will become scarcer and more expensive in future. Arguments of this kind have been used to support highly ambitious plans to double the area of commercial forestry – the Forestry Commission themselves consider that with due allowance for other interests there are still about 1.1 million ha of rough grazing land suitable for planting.

These targets are most unlikely to be met. Land in the hills is becoming more expensive and difficult to acquire, partly because the economics of sheep farming have improved somewhat under new CAP arrangements. The actual rate of new planting will depend heavily on the Forestry Commission's budget and the extent of grants and subsidies available to private investors, whom the Government would like to take a bigger share in afforestation. Furthermore, there is likely to be strong opposition to planting on many sites, especially on environmental grounds. Over half the area otherwise suitable for planting in England and Wales falls within designated sites – National Parks, Areas of Outstanding Natural Beauty, and SSSIs. Even the most limited increases in afforestation will produce head-on collisions with other land uses.

With both activities dependent on heavy subsidies, there is much debate about whether the uplands are more productively employed in agriculture or commercial forestry. It is frequently argued that forestry and associated timber industries can generate more jobs in the hills than farming and this alleged benefit is often referred to in government statements. The foundations of this argument are, however, somewhat insecure. Mechanisation has meant fewer jobs and even these have become increasingly expensive to create. New jobs could be created in tourism and recreation at a lower cost and it is notable that no recent government has shown enthusiasm for building up a more robust wood-processing industry in the hills.

While grazing sheep in the uplands produces a low, but relatively predictable, return, timber production is a highly speculative business, even with fast-growing softwoods which may be felled 40–60 years after planting. Everything depends on the volume of future demand in Britain and the level of world timber prices, both of which are extremely difficult to predict. Most forecasts assume that Britain's demand for wood products will rise inexorably and that eventually our hunger for timber will be confronted by a severe world shortage, predicted in one authoritative forecast to transpire around 2020–2030. This kind of statement invites disbelief and there is a tendency for these forecasts to be based on rather unsophisticated economic analyses and display an almost sentimental attachment to 1960s style economic growth. There are many reasons for thinking that Britain's wood demands may rise very little in future; the growth in telecommunications may limit any rise in paper demand, for example, and a major rise in pulp prices would provide a big incentive for paper recycling. Less than 30% of British paper is recovered, a worse performance than any other Western country outside the US.

Future timber prices are unpredictable because so many factors are involved, but they undoubtedly have a great bearing on forestry economics. One recent study of four areas of North Wales suggested that, with stable wood prices, 19% of the area would be planted, but at the other extreme, a price rise of 3½% a year in real terms would make about 85% of the area plantable. With so much at stake improved models of future timber markets are imperative and in the meantime claims that conifer plantations will produce a good return should be treated with scepticism. Forestry already benefits from a lower disincentive than other forms of public investment (3% rather than 5), and there is some doubt about its ability to meet this target. Conifers on exposed sites, for example in the Western Isles of Scotland, are vulnerable to windthrow and some commentators claim that the Forestry Commission have failed to anticipate this problem and that it will necessitate shorter rotations and lower yields. In short, almost every aspect of forestry economics is open to dispute and the urgency of further planting is somewhat undermined by the fact that the present area of trees, when in sustained yield, could provide about half our present need for wood products.

Commercial forestry has become associated with an alien

invasion because it usually takes the form of large blocks of even-aged, closely planted and usually coniferous trees. Until fairly recently these blocks were often planted with little regard for the local land-form, producing hard geometric lines and tending to smother the landscape. Landscaping and design are now more sensitive, but to the majority of people who seek pleasure and recreation in the hills large conifer plantations are an unwelcome intrusion. For wildlife too, the impact of afforestation is on balance negative. Detailed studies of the environmental impact of upland afforestation are by no means numerous but there are many areas of concern, including the long-term effects on soil quality and future production, the impact of new planting on water yields, the effects of altered water regimes, including chemical changes in runoff water and the effects of increased use of pesticides and fertilizers.

These threats could be much reduced by different forms of forestry, notably the planting of deciduous species on suitable land both in the lowlands and in the hills. At present less than 10% of new planting is of broadleaved trees. Although grants are more generous than for conifers, the long rotations and uncertain returns ensure that fewer people consider broadleaves capable of producing a commercial return. Indeed, when broadleaves are felled they are frequently replaced by conifers or mixed plantations and this has been the fate of many ancient semi-natural woods. The area of broadleaves is declining, old oakwoods in particular are disappearing and where new woodland is springing up it is often birch, sycamore and ash or scrub which has escaped felling or grazing, rather than managed forest.

The protection of remaining broadleaved woodlands is now an urgent priority, especially in the lowlands. They are valuable not only for landscape and wildlife, but for recreation and education and with appropriate management many woods could produce a useful timber yield. Since many are in danger of being converted to conifers or felled and ploughed, with grants payable towards the cost of both, their protection demands changes in both forestry and agricultural policy and a positive programme of advice, information where necessary, and financial aid for their owners. Once again, the extension of planning controls over forestry might greatly assist conservation.

And Finally . . .

There has been space here to look at only a few of the major land uses in Britain. There are many others of environmental concern, for example the continuing practice of waste disposal authorities of ridding themselves of 85% of waste, most of it untreated, by landfill. We can also expect entirely new and sometimes unwelcome uses of land. A graphic example of this was a recent claim by the Town and Country Planning Association that the volume of low level radioactive waste which might accumulate in Britain over the next century could be as much as 3.85 million cubic metres, enough to fill a ditch one metre deep from London to Moscow. For intermediate level waste, at a mere 611,000 cubic metres, the trench would only reach as far as Edinburgh!

Further Reading

Best, R. H. 1981, *Land Use and Living Space*, Methuen.
Centre for Agricultural Strategy 1980, *Strategy for the UK Forestry Industry*, CAS Report 6.
The Conservation and Development Programme for the UK 1983. A Response to the World Conservation Strategy, Kogan Page.
Council for the Protection of Rural England 1981, *Planning – Friend or Foe?*, CPRE.
Forestry Commission 1977, *The Wood Production Outlook in Britain – A Review*, The Forestry Commission.
King, A. and Conroy, C. 1981, *Paradise Lost?*, FoE.
Mabey, R. 1981, *The Common Ground: A Place for Nature in Britain's Future?*, Hutchinson.
MacEwen, A. and M. 1982, *National Parks: Conservation or Cosmetics?*, George Allen and Unwin.
Ministry of Agriculture, Fisheries and Food (annually), *Annual Review of Agriculture*, HMSO.
Newby, H. 1980, *Green and Pleasant Land?*, Penguin.
Northfield, L. (Chairman) 1979, *Report of the Committee of Inquiry into the Acquisition and Occupancy of Agricultural Land*, HMSO.
Norton-Taylor, R. 1982, *Whose Land is it Anyway?*, Turnstone Press.

BRIAN PRICE

5 Pollution: 'The invisible violence'

A SUITABLY EQUIPPED alien observer landing
virtually anywhere on the planet Earth would be able to detect the
existence of an extraordinary species – humanity – by the analysis of
air, water and biological samples, even though the nearest human
settlement might be hundreds of kilometres away. Variations in the
amounts of metals in polar snow and ice of different ages, the presence
in animal tissues of chemicals rarely if every found in nature, and
even levels of acid in falling rain not explainable by normal biological
or geological processes – all these would point to the presence of an
organism capable of extracting, processing and mobilising materials
to an extent not achievable by ordinary species.

This is not to suggest that human activities have damaged
every square centimetre of the globe, but it does show that our waste
products are globally distributed. For the most part the elevations in
levels of natural materials and the injection of small amounts of
synthetic substances into the environment cause little harm.
However, in some localities and in some vital global systems serious
harm is being caused or is likely to occur, some of it possibly
irreversible.

There is a common misconception that all pollution is caused by artificial materials, implying a distinction in potential hazard between natural and synthetic substances. In fact, natural poisons frequently can surpass in nastiness the chemist's creations and some of the most serious pollution problems result not from exotic synthetics but from natural chemicals in the wrong places and/or at too high concentrations.

Cycles involving physical, chemical, geological and biological processes control the distribution and fates of natural materials in the environment. Pollution can result when these are overloaded or otherwise disrupted by humans – as when too much sewage for breakdown processes to cope with is pumped into a stream. Persistent synthetic compounds, i.e. those which do not break down readily, complicate the picture when there are no natural cycles to deal with them. Special problems of accumulations in living organisms may then occur, as with the insecticide DDT which had devasting effects on wildlife in the 1950s and 1960s.

It may not always be obvious that a natural cycle is being disrupted since there are scanty data about the concentrations of many substances in the environment and the way these concentrations vary naturally. Predicting the effects of disturbances in these concentrations and variations is particularly difficult. A case in point is the controversy over the levels of carbon dioxide in the atmosphere. Carbon dioxide is a gas produced by the respiration of organisms and the decomposition of organic matter. It is present naturally in the air at a low concentration but over the past hundred years or so this concentration has been increasing. The reason for this is principally the combustion of fossil fuels, the carbon in which is converted into carbon dioxide. Natural 'sinks' for carbon dioxide exist – the sea dissolves it and plants use it during photosynthesis – but fuel combustion is releasing the gas faster than it can be removed from the atmosphere.

Carbon dioxide has a property of vital importance to the control of the earth's climate. It absorbs heat which would otherwise be radiated away and, as a result, the atmosphere warms up, the extent of this warming increasing as carbon dioxide levels rise.

This much is generally accepted but the controversy centres around how much of an atmospheric temperature increase is likely to result from a given rise in carbon dioxide concentration, and the probable consequences of such an increase. Other atmospheric gases, e.g. methane, are involved in global temperature control and it is not clear how large their roles are.

The earth's climate would certainly be affected if the

temperature rose and because any rise would be larger at higher latitudes than at the equator the winds and ocean currents which control rainfall patterns would be changed. Some deserts could become arable lands while the main wheat-growing areas of North America could become arid and virtually useless, resulting in widespread changes in world agriculture. A warmer global climate could also cause the melting of ice at the poles, drowning many of the world's cities which lie at or near sea level. A considerable amount of research into the carbon dioxide problem is currently underway and for the moment the likely consequences of our profligate use of fossil fuels remain unclear. However, it has been suggested seriously by some experts that it would be folly to continue burning fossil fuels in our current wasteful manner if we are to avoid undesirable climatic changes – another reason, if one were needed, for energy conservation.

Another gaseous pollutant which results from the combustion of oil and coal is sulphur dioxide. This is one of a group of substances responsible for a phenomenon known as acid rain which is currently wreaking havoc on ecosystems in several countries. Again, the scientific details are unclear, with experts disagreeing about the causes and seriousness of acid rain.

Acid rain was first identified during the 1960s by researchers in Sweden and Norway who were concerned about the increasing acidity of many Scandinavian lakes and the death of fish therein. During the 1970s they became convinced that the deposition of acidic materials in rain and snowfall was the main cause. The lakes in question are particularly susceptible to the effects of acid since the rocks surrounding and below them contain no limestone to act as a neutralising agent. Thus, repeated doses of acid cause the waters to become highly acidic and this causes the dissolution of metals from the underlying rocks, including aluminium which is highly toxic to fish under the conditions described. Fish populations in some 9,000 Swedish lakes have suffered varying degrees of damage, many of them dying out completely. Although Scandinavia was first to be affected, a conference in West Germany in 1983 was told that every country in Western Europe is now suffering.

The principal gas involved is sulphur dioxide which dissolves in water to form acid. It is emitted naturally by volcanoes but in most areas the largest source is the combustion of fuels containing sulphur, particularly in large power stations. The emissions from such plants, and from some other industrial sites, can travel long distances. In Scandinavia most of the sulphur dioxide damaging the lakes originates outside the countries concerned.

The other important acidic gases are the oxides of nitrogen which are formed during high-temperature combustion processes. Again, power stations are important sources but other processes can be highly significant. Motor vehicles emit oxides of nitrogen which are partly responsible for the smogs afflicting heavily-trafficked sunny cities such as Los Angeles, Athens and Sydney. West Germany has now announced strict control measures on the emission of nitrogen oxides from vehicles in response to the threat to its national forests believed to come from acid rain.

The situation is, inevitably, more complicated than described above. There is uncertainty about the contributions made to acidification by the different compounds involved and by the substances into which they are changed by chemical processes in the environment. Some of the acidity arrives in the form of dissolved gases in rain and snow while some is caused by dry acidic particles – hence the term 'acid precipitation' is more accurate than 'acid rain'. The sources of the various components, too, are often unclear. In some areas – including parts of the United Kingdom – acidification appears to be occurring in lakes but the amounts of acid involved do not tally with the amounts falling in precipitation. Many scientists now believe that we cannot wait any longer for a completely clear picture of causes and effects for it is apparent that many Scandinavian lakes are suffering badly from acid rain and large tracts of forest in Europe and North America are under threat.

The most appropriate control strategy for acid rain will vary from country to country, depending on the contributions made by the different sources of acid, climatic factors and other variables. In some countries it may be best to remove sulphur from fuels before they are burned, while in others cleaner burning techniques, such as fluidised bed combustion, may be most suitable. Sweden has already imposed strict limits on the sulphur content of fuels burned in large plants and is calling on other European countries to do the same.

One of the key scientific arguments has been whether or not a reduction in sulphur emissions would bring about an equivalent reduction in acid deposition – the suggestion being that it may be more appropriate to control other gases. Britain has used this argument to oppose demands from the Swedes to reduce its emissions but a report from the US National Academy of Sciences, published in 1983, supported the view that reducing sulphur emissions would be effective.

The question of acid rain has become a major political issue in Europe. Britain is widely regarded as a major source of the acid reaching Scandinavia and, in a clever ploy to deflect pressure for improvements, the National Coal Board and the Central Electricity Generating Board announced, in September 1983, their funding of a £5 million research project into Scandinavian acidification. This was viewed with some annoyance by the Swedes and Norwegians who would have much preferred action to yet more research. Despite the arguments as to how bad acid rain is and who is responsible, one point is absolutely clear. Acid deposition is an international problem which cannot be solved by single countries in isolation. Pollution of this kind is no respecter of national boundaries.

Nitrogen oxides, as has been mentioned, enter the atmosphere as a result of combustion processes. Another, but unquantified, mechanism is via the action of bacteria on the nitrogen fertilizers used to increase crop yields. The best recognised hazards of these materials, however, are in the sphere of water, rather than atmospheric pollution.

Nitrogen fertilizers can promote the growth of water plants just as readily as farmers' crops and when they are washed into streams by the rain, a massive overgrowth of algae (small water plants) can occur. These overgrowths, or 'blooms' blanket the stream or pond leaving bottom-living plants without vital light. Dead bottom plants, and eventually the remains of the algae, decompose under the influence of bacteria and as this happens all the oxygen dissolved in the water is used up, resulting in a foul-smelling and lifeless watercourse. This process is called eutrophication and is most serious in lakes, although it can also be a problem in slow-flowing rivers.

For eutrophication to occur, adequate supplies of phosphates must be present as well as nitrates. Phosphates, too, are used as fertilizers and can cause run-off problems although domestic sewage is usually a more important source. Sewage also contains large quantities of nitrates, the exact concentration depending on the degree of treatment to which it has been subjected before being discharged. The phosphate content of sewage comes partly from the breakdown of waste matter and partly from the use of phosphates as water softeners in washing powders.

More serious than the problem of eutrophication is the potential hazard, particularly to young babies, posed by rising levels of nitrates in drinking water. Nitrates are converted by bacteria in the human gut into nitrites, related substances which can combine with the oxygen-carrying pigment in the blood. If this happens to an excessive degree, a condition called methaemoglobinaemia results in which the victim effectively suffocates from within as the blood cannot carry adequate oxygen for the body's needs. Babies are particularly at risk since they have more of the necessary bacteria in their guts than do adults.

Methaemoglobinaemia is currently not very common in the developed world – some thousand cases have been recorded in Europe with about 8% proving fatal – but nitrate levels in rivers used for water supply are increasing, sometimes alarmingly, and with them the risk that more people may be affected. Already mothers of young babies have been supplied with bottled low-nitrate water for use in making up feeds in parts of Britain where levels in tap water have reached unacceptable values. In 1976 some two million people in East Anglia received water through their taps with more than the World Health Organisation's recommended limit for nitrates.

On average, about half the nitrates in river water arrive there as a result of sewage discharges and half come from agriculture, although the balance will vary from river to river. It is not only rivers that are affected: groundwater sources are threatened by nitrate pollution as well. Some fertilizer residues can percolate through the soil and, where permeable water-containing rocks (aquifers) underly the surface, contamination of potential water supplies can result. Furthermore, the ploughing up of large areas of permanent pasture in Southern England during and after the Second World War released large quantities of nitrates from the surface layers of the soil. These are still on their way down towards water supplies – a phenomenon dubbed by some scientists as the 'nitrate time bomb'.

The existence of a nitrate time bomb has been the subject of some scientific dispute but a draft report by the Standing Technical Advisory Committee on Water Quality, prepared in 1982, demonstrated that in much of southern England a serious situation exists and also that the contribution of fertilizers to rising nitrate levels in many rivers is increasing.

There is a further problem posed by nitrates in water for human consumption, which may affect adults as well as infants. It has been suggested that nitrates can be converted in the gut, by a series of chemical reactions, into substances called N-nitrosamines. N-nitrosamines are thought to cause cancer of the stomach and therefore rising levels of nitrates in drinking water could increase the incidence of this disease. Nitrates in the diet are derived from a number of sources but water is a major one, and is likely to become increasingly significant as levels rise.

There are other materials which harm children more readily than adults. Lead is prominent among such pollutants. For thousands of years lead has been used by humans for such purposes as pipes, vessels, paints, cosmetics and solders. For almost as long, its toxic effects have been appreciated, with cases of lead poisoning documented in Roman times. Few people now suffer from acute lead poisoning, although every year in Britain dozens of children who have eaten lead paint are admitted to hospital. Of greater concern are the effects of much lower lead exposures on the mental development of a large proportion of our children.

Lead is a neurotoxin – it attacks the nerves and brain – and it has been known for nearly four decades that children who have 'recovered' from lead poisoning may still be left with permanent brain damage. Less easy to demonstrate has been the damage to children's brains caused by levels of lead which do not produce obvious symptoms of poisoning – levels to which children are exposed routinely in the environment.

Intensive research in the 1970s and early 1980s amassed a considerable weight of evidence suggesting that current lead exposures do, in fact, cause harm. One of the most important pieces of work was carried out by Dr Herbert Needleman in Boston, USA. Needleman measured the lead levels in the shed milk teeth of children and compared the results with assessments made by teachers of each child's IQ and behaviour in the classroom. He found (after allowing for some 37 factors not related to lead) that those children having high lead levels in their teeth did significantly less well in the tests than did those with low levels. The importance of this is that the lead levels regarded as high are common in city children – a point which led Dr Robert Stephens, of Birmingham University, to conclude that some 20% of British urban children are likely to be suffering from some form of lead-induced mental impairment.

The case against lead at low levels of exposure is not completely conclusive and a few studies have produced conflicting or ambivalent results. Absolute proof of cause and effect in this field is rarely, if ever, obtained and the only prudent conclusion which can be drawn from the data available is that a significant number of our young children are affected by low-level lead – a conclusion which successive British governments studiously and cynically avoided drawing for over a decade. These effects take the form of slight mental impairment, behavioural difficulties and learning problems, perhaps equivalent to a reduction in IQ of a few points.

The source of the lead causing this damage is as controversial a topic as the existence of the damage itself. The general population is exposed to lead from a variety of sources including emissions from motor vehicles, lead pipes carrying drinking water, paint, food contaminated by lead in soil and air and also some forms of industrial pollution. The relative importance of the different sources varies from place to place. In some areas, soft water running through long stretches of lead pipe contributes the major proportion of human lead intake while in other places the inhalation of lead particles emitted by motor vehicles and the ingestion of dust contaminated by the same source pose the greatest hazard.

The debate about the hazards of lead has focused primarily on the emissions of the metal from motor vehicles. Until recently the official view – as embodied in the report of the DHSS's Lawther Committee on Lead and Health – was that lead from petrol contributed only a minor amount to the total intake, except in some people living very close to heavily trafficked roads. The main flaw in this assumption is that it considered only directly-inhaled traffic lead while the contamination of food, cooking surfaces and utensils, and dust likely to be ingested by children, was largely overlooked. When these factors are taken into account, a different picture is obtained with vehicle lead frequently constituting the largest single source of contamination.

Several recent studies have supported the view that petrol is a major source of bodily lead. In 1979 Dr I. H. Billick, of the US Department of Housing and Urban Development, showed that the levels of lead in New York children varied according to the amount of lead in petrol sold in the city – when the amount of petrol lead sold increased, so did blood lead levels and a decline in petrol lead sales was followed by a decline in blood lead. Further evidence came in 1982 from a study by the Center for Disease Control in Atlanta which showed that a drop of 37% in the average blood lead levels of US citizens during the period 1977–1980 could be correlated with a drop in the amount of lead used in petrol of about a half.

Lead is added to petrol to improve its performance in high compression engines. No one disputes the fact that motor cars can run on unleaded petrol or that suitable petrol can be made without the use of lead. The main dispute is about the costs, to industry and the motorist, of doing so. Making lead-free high octane (4-star) petrol would involve the oil industry in extra capital and refining costs while making cars to run on low-octane lead-free petrol would involve extra costs for the car manufacturers. For these reasons, the industries involved have strenuously resisted attempts to prohibit the use of lead in petrol, claiming that it would be vastly expensive to do so and would not be worth the extra costs involved. It is significant that oil company estimates of the costs of reducing petrol lead in West Germany, and of banning it in Australia, proved to be gross overestimates.

The question of lead in the environment was investigated by the Royal Commission on Environmental Pollution whose ninth report, published in 1983, contained a wide-ranging set of recommendations. The RCEP felt that, on balance, the benefits of banning the use of lead in petrol outweighed the costs and recommended accordingly. It also called for drastic reductions in the amount of lead used in paint and for the speedy removal of dangerous lead plumbing in buildings. Although the RCEP report was inconclusive on whether lead damages young children at the levels claimed by the metal's opponents, it endorsed the general principle that it is unwise to distribute a material exhibiting the toxicity and persistence of lead throughout the environment in such quantities as are currently permitted.

The British Government responded to the sections concerning lead in petrol within hours of the report's publication. The Secretary of State for the Environment accepted the recommendations but did not set a firm timetable for the introduction of lead-free petrol, a matter of some concern to campaigners. At the time of writing, negotiations are underway with the petrol companies, the motor manufacturers, and the rest of the EEC to establish timetables and mechanisms for implementing the RCEP's recommendations. Meanwhile, West Germany has announced that all new cars sold after January 1st 1986 must run on lead-free fuel.

Lead is one member of a group of substances known as the heavy metals. Several others in this group have caused serious pollution problems, in the UK and elsewhere. Like lead, they are present in the environment naturally at low levels and it is only when these levels are boosted much above normal, usually by human activities, that problems occur.

A second problematical heavy metal is cadmium, which causes heart problems, kidney damage, lung disease and possibly cancer when absorbed by humans via different routes. It is used industrially in metal plating, alloys, pigments and batteries and is also finding increasing use in the microelectronics field. Effluents from some of these processes, particularly small plating works, frequently find their way into domestic sewers and supplement the cadmium contributed by human wastes. As a result, the sewage sludge produced at water treatment plants can contain high levels of cadmium which restrict its use as a fertilizer on agricultural land.

Ordinary phosphate fertilizers contain varying amounts of cadmium which is present in the rocks whence they are derived and their use can lead to a build-up of cadmium in soils. The manufacture of these fertilizers generates large quantities of cadmium-containing wastes, much of which are currently dumped at sea, a practice being opposed vigorously by the environmental group Greenpeace.

The release of cadmium from smelting operations has caused the build-up of high levels in the Severn Estuary such that local environmental health officers have recommended that no one should eat more than four ounces of shellfish from the estuary per week. Meanwhile, residents in the adjacent Somerset village of Shipham have been screened for the adverse effects of cadmium following the discovery of high levels of the metal in local soils and streams as a result of long-abandoned zinc mines. No serious health problems were demonstrated in the inhabitants of Shipham, but monitoring continues and the consumption of some home-grown vegetables is officially discouraged.

A third heavy metal, mercury, has wreaked havoc on humans and wildlife in the past and still presents hazards today. In the 1950s, in the Japanese Minamata Bay, the discharge of mercury-laden industrial effluents led to the build-up of mercury in fish and consequently many cases of deformity and death occurred in the villagers who ate the fish. Damage to wildlife by mercury-based fungicides resulted in those materials being banned in Sweden in the 1960s and severely restricted elsewhere, while a massive outbreak of poisoning occurred in Iraq following the consumption of bread made from seed grain treated with mercury fungicides.

Mercury levels in some British coastal waters, notably Liverpool Bay, are greatly elevated as a result of industrial effluents and the dumping of sewage sludge. In the Thames estuary, however, mercury levels in water and fish have been reduced considerably in recent years following a vigorous clampdown by the water authority on the discharge of mercury from industrial premises into the sewers.

Since the heavy metals are elements they cannot be destroyed but can only be combined with other elements. Some of these combinations can result in the removal of metals from the environment – e.g. in deep sea sediments – but when removal mechanisms are overloaded the amounts of metals available to living things increase. When the metal is particularly toxic problems can occur since organisms which have evolved against a low natural background level of the material cannot always cope with the elevated levels.

Another material of mineral origin which has proved harmful

is asbestos. Several forms of asbestos exist, known as blue, white and brown in accordance with their approximate colours. All types of asbestos have been used widely for a variety of industrial and domestic purposes for many years since their properties of inertness, resistance to chemical attack and very low heat conductivity have proved invaluable.

The use of asbestos, however, has left a dreadful legacy of disease in people who have mined and handled it and it still presents very serious hazards despite new controls on its use. Two medical conditions are caused by asbestos: asbestosis and mesothelioma. Asbestosis is a painful, debilitating disease which results from the inhalation of large quantities of asbestos fibres. The lungs progressively clog up, exertion becomes difficult, breathing becomes more and more painful and death usually ensues. Mesothelioma is a fatal cancer of the inner chest wall caused only by the inhalation of asbestos. A single exposure to the material is sufficient and one does not have to work with it to be at risk – a case was recorded in a woman whose only contact was asbestos tipped on a waste dump near her home.

The hazards of asbestos have been recognised for decades but it was many years before compensation became payable to workers injured by the material, and still longer before even partially adequate controls were imposed on it. Yet current industrial safety standards are regarded by some experts as being far too lax – the latest revisions will still permit the deaths of many workers exposed to white asbestos for long periods.

The general public may be exposed to asbestos from a variety of sources. Many domestic items, such as ironing boards, ovens and electrical heating equipment, have contained asbestos in the past and some still do. Asbestos sheeting has been used for roofs and walls and the material is also used in pipes, floor tiles and textured finishes for ceilings. Many council houses, hospitals and other public buildings contain asbestos insulation while the lagging used in old power stations was nearly always asbestos. The Central Electricity Generating Board's practice of selling off old power stations to private contractors with the asbestos lagging intact was roundly condemned on safety grounds following the release of asbestos into the air during the demolition of Fulham power station in 1983. Campaigning by FoE and concerned residents' groups forced the Board to change its policy.

Since asbestos cannot be destroyed, its disposal presents serious problems. The safest place for it is back in the ground whence it came but getting it there is difficult. Solid asbestos sheet is not particularly dangerous but when asbestos is crushed, scraped, drilled or otherwise handled roughly, fibres are released into the atmosphere and health hazards are created. The safe removal of asbestos is a highly skilled job and operatives have to wear space-suit style protective clothing and extremely efficient respirators.

Asbestos is, of course, not the only hazardous waste which has to be disposed of in the UK. Many industrial and commercial processes produce wastes which are either toxic, polluting, inflammable, explosive or otherwise dangerous. The problems of the safe disposal of hazardous wastes were highlighted in the early 1970s when a series of incidents, culminating in the discovery of drums of cyanide dumped on land used as a playground by children in the Midlands, forced the Government of the day to bring in emergency legislation. Even now, controls on hazardous wastes are not completely effective and incidents of wastes going to the wrong place, leaking, catching fire, exploding or simply 'disappearing' still occur. The House of Lords Select Committee on Science and Technology, in its 1981 report on hazardous wastes, identified a number of deficiencies in the British system of control and although the Government has reacted positively to some of the committee's recommendations, other problems remain unresolved. In particular, the Department of the Environment seems to be bowing to pressure from industry to ignore the recommendation that all handlers of hazardous waste should be licensed – at the moment, anyone with an old lorry can set up in the business without training or experience.

Amazingly, the total amount of hazardous waste produced in the UK is not known accurately, partly because there is no completely satisfactory definition covering it. According to one classification, some five million or so tonnes per year are involved but Harwell, the principal Government research body considering hazardous waste, admitted to the Select Committee that it did not know how much the UK produces, who is responsible, what specifically it constitutes, and what happens to it.

The main means of waste disposal in Britain is landfill, i.e. the material is dumped in a hole in the ground with a greater or lesser degree of care according to the diligence of the site operator and the vigilance of the local authority monitoring it. Some wastes can be recycled, recovering valuable materials, while others can be burned as fuels. The toxic or other harmful properties of some wastes can be destroyed by chemical means – occasionally by using one waste to neutralise another – and it is also possible to immobilise various materials in a sort of synthetic rock before landfilling, thereby reducing the likelihood of the waste escaping from the tip in harmful quantities.

There is no national toxic waste management policy to control what happens to hazardous materials and ensure that the best environmental option is used for their disposal. The Department of the Environment can give advice (and in the case of some types of waste the Secretary of State can direct that they go to a specific site), and local authorities can control the types and quantities of wastes disposed of on tips in their own areas, but there is no means of ensuring that, say, solvents are recovered or burned safely rather than being dumped in a hole.

While the current management of hazardous waste is unsatis-factory, the handling of wastes in the past has, on occasions, been positively scandalous. Wastes of all types have been dumped in an uncontrolled manner on unsuitable sites and records of the materials involved have frequently not been kept. Some such sites have been identified, and even restored, but many remain undocumented and some are undoubtedly yet to be rediscovered. When these sites are disturbed or reactivated, the consequences can be dramatic – one old tip in South Wales is now leaking toxic solvents into a stream passing beside a new housing estate, while in Ealing, West London, residents of the Willow Tree Lane Estate have complained of sickness and skin irritation from wastes thought to have been dumped there several decades previously.

Some of the wastes dumped in the ground will become harmless in time as natural chemical and biological processes break them down. Others, like the heavy metals and some synthetic compounds, remain hazardous indefinitely and provision must be made for their isolation from the environment for very long periods. Two philosophies on waste disposal exist, abbreviated to 'dilute and disperse' and 'concentrate and contain'. In the former case, wastes are theoretically released slowly from disposal sites so that they are well diluted before they reach water supplies or sensitive wildlife. In the latter, the most hazardous materials are kept in some form of containment from which they should never escape. In practice, there are drawbacks to both approaches so compromises have to be sought. If persistent wastes are dispersed, for instance, biological processes can sometimes reconcentrate them to dangerous levels, while ensuring that they can never escape from a 'concentrate and contain' site is virtually impossible.

One of the factors given most weight in deciding whether or

not a site can be used for waste disposal is the protection of ground-water resources which could be polluted by materials leaching downwards from the site. In the USA many wells have recently been found to be contaminated by toxic and cancer-causing chemicals dumped in unsuitable places and water abstraction from some of them has had to be halted.

The problem of low-level contamination of water supplies by a variety of chemicals is also becoming important in Britain. Traces of solvents such as chloroform, pesticides, drugs such as the contra-ceptive pill and various other materials – collectively known as organic micropollutants – are beginning to give water authorities headaches. Some of these materials are produced by the action of chlorine (added at waterworks to kill bacteria) on traces of compounds already contaminating the water, while others are there as a result of the extraction of water from rivers receiving agricultural run-off, industrial discharges and sewage containing materials not destroyed by normal treatment processes. So far, no health effects have been attributed positively to these organic micropollutants in the UK but as their concentrations and variety increase concern is growing, particularly as some of the chemicals concerned can cause cancer.

It is not only industrial wastes which are capable of causing pollution: those from agriculture can be just as bad. The slurry from intensive livestock units and silage liquors have become increasingly important river pollutants in recent years, particularly in the south-west of England. These wastes have very high Biochemical Oxygen Demands (BODs) which means that they easily deoxygenate the waters into which they are discharged, resulting in a malodorous and lifeless waterway. However, the pollutants of agricultural origin which cause most public concern are largely synthetic compounds – pesticides.

The harmful effects of pesticides on people and the environment were first documented by Rachel Carson over two decades ago in her classic book *Silent Spring*. Despite strenuous efforts by the industry to discredit the book and its author, the ensuing furore forced some governments to curb the worst excesses of pesticide use. However, a state of complacency now exists, in British Government circles at least, despite the fact that pesticides still present serious problems.

The term 'pesticide' includes all materials designed to kill animals and plants which compete with humans for food and land or affect stored produce, structures or human health. In Britain, the majority of pesticides are used in agriculture but in other countries the use of insecticides in public health programmes, such as malaria control, is of great importance.

The main classes of pesticides are insecticides, used against insects and similar invertebrates; herbicides, used against weeds; and fungicides, used against fungi which cause diseases in crops and rot wood. As a general rule, insecticides are more toxic to higher animals, including humans, than are herbicides and fungicides although there some exceptions, notably the herbicide paraquat and certain mercury-based fungicides.

The most notorious insecticides are those in the organochlorine group which includes DDT, dieldrin and HCH. These substances are slow to break down in the environment and may be accumulated to high levels in the tissues of organisms exposed to them. Residues can then be passed on to creatures feeding on the first organisms and there have been many cases of predators such as owls, hawks and even otters suffering ill effects as a result. During the 1950s and early 1960s populations of peregrine falcons declined dramatically as a result of the careless use of dieldrin which also played a part in the decline of the British otter.

Not all insecticides are as unpleasantly persistent as the organo-chlorine group, but break down fairly quickly in the environment. Before they do so, however, they are quite capable of causing harm to wildlife and even humans. Most insecticides are fairly indiscriminate in their effects and can wipe out populations of harmless insects, as well as killing higher animals such as fish, birds and mammals which happen to stray under the spray or into recently treated areas. Where affected non-target insects are predators of the pest causing the problem, the situation can be made worse since natural controls on the numbers of that pest are thereby weakened. Furthermore, many pests are now resistant to the commoner insecticides, a problem of alarming significance in the public health context.

Human fatalities from the use of pesticides are rare in the UK but common in the developing world. In a powerful book by David Bull called *A Growing Problem*, Oxfam has documented literally thousands of incidents of pesticide poisoning in Third World countries where there are few safety regulations and little control on the types of pesticides used. Deplorably, British and American companies are often responsible for selling these chemicals, several of which are banned in the developed world.

Insecticides are not the only pesticides causing problems. The use of herbicides as part of modern intensive farming has had devastating effects on our wild flora and fauna. Once common species are now rare. Residues of paraquat, an increasingly popular but highly toxic herbicide, have frequently proved fatal to hares eating treated stubble; this is thought to be one of the factors responsible for the decline of these animals. The substance 2,4,5-T is even more controversial since it is thought to cause cancers and birth defects in people exposed to it. The United States banned many of 2,4,5-T's uses, following suggestions that it may have caused miscarriages in Oregon, and the American courts are currently considering claims by veterans of the Vietnam war who believe that their health was seriously and permanently affected when 2,4,5-T was used to defoliate parts of Vietnam. Swedish studies found that workers using 2,4,5-T and similar substances have a seven times greater chance of developing certain types of cancer than comparable workers not using the chemicals. You can buy 2,4,5-T in your local garden shop since the British authorities do not accept the evidence against it.

It is a little uncertain whether the effects of 2,4,5-T are caused by the pesticide itself or a contaminant, inevitably present as a result of the manufacturing process, called dioxin (TCDD). Dioxin is one of the most toxic materials ever synthesised and was responsible for widespread harm after the accident at the Seveso chemical works, near Milan, in 1976. The disposal of the waste from the accident caused a political storm in 1983 when the company responsible refused to say what had happened to it. It eventually turned up in a French butcher's shed and was then sent to Switzerland for incineration. Britain had its own dioxin scandal in 1968, when an explosion at a Coalite chemical factory in Derbyshire generated a considerable quantity of dioxin waste. The whereabouts of this material is only vaguely known and even now Coalite refuse to say what happened to the dioxin-contaminated wastes produced during the plant's normal operation.

Many countries have strict legislation regulating the sale and use of pesticides but, in Britain, most of the controls are voluntary. The system does not seem to be working, however, since much more DDT is used than should be under the official agreement; safety precautions and restrictions on such matters as the storage and use of toxic compounds are widely ignored; and in the summer of 1983 fish – and possibly otters – were dying in English rivers following the use of dieldrin in sheep dips theoretically banned years previously.

A worldwide campaign against the environmentally unacceptable use of pesticides is now underway, with Friends of the Earth playing the leading role in the UK. The first targets in the

British campaign are the secrecy with which pesticide safety data are treated and the non-statutory nature of the control mechanisms.

A major problem associated with many of the pollution issues discussed above is lack of information. In some cases this is simply a result of human ignorance – we do not find out what effects a substance or practice has on the environment until it becomes widespread. This may be a legacy of the past where the effects of an entrenched technology only become apparent after many years, or it may be simply the result of inadequate testing of new substances or processes.

Perhaps more sinister is the deliberate suppression of information by those in the know, notably the authorities who are supposed to protect us. Information on the toxicity of pesticides, hazardous industrial processes, the storage of dangerous chemicals in bulk, pollution emissions to the air and many other such matters is kept confidential between industry and Government. In 1974, Parliament passed the Control of Pollution Act, part of which required water authorities to maintain a register of discharges to their rivers. Ten years later this section is still not properly in force, prevarication by industry and bureaucrats having caused the delay. Other sections also remain to be implemented.

The availability of information is only one factor hindering the fight against pollution. Of course, more research is needed in some areas and more data should be available to the concerned citizen who wants to take an active part. But even where the facts are known, or the evidence concerning a particular problem is sufficiently strong to merit action, Governments are slow to act. Once a substance or process is in daily use, it is regarded, all too often, as innocent until proven guilty. Those wishing to tighten controls usually have to make a watertight case – generally on a shoestring budget – since Government departments are reluctant to impose constraints on industry unless forced to do so.

Some pollution problems have obvious solutions – lead burdens in the general population, for instance, could readily be reduced by a swift ban on the use of lead in petrol. With others there may be no easy answers – for example, nothing can be done to prevent the nitrates percolating down through rock strata from reaching groundwater and expensive treatment at waterworks will probably be necessary.

Cost is frequently the deciding factor in pollution controversies – opponents of change claim that it would be more expensive to adopt alternative practices. Yet these arguments are only valid in the short term. It may cost industry slightly more to dispose of its wastes in a safer manner but – as the Americans have found with their legacy of leaking toxic dumps – it can cost vastly more to clean up dangerous old tips or decontaminate a water supply. It would undoubtedly cost the CEGB money to reduce sulphur dioxide emissions from its power stations, but the Organisation for Economic Co-operation and Development (OECD) has reported that the benefits of reducing the effects of acid rain would outweigh the costs of a Europe-wide sulphur dioxide clean-up.

Of course, not all the costs of pollution can be put in terms of cash. How, for instance, does one put a price on a child's intellect or the health of a population? What is the financial value of our wildlife heritage? Simple calculations of costs versus benefits in the field of pollution control are frequently inadequate but they are sometimes used with a spurious air of validity.

This short chapter has provided a snapshot view of some major pollution problems, mainly from a British standpoint. Of necessity, the issues have been simplified, discussion abbreviated and some topics omitted altogether. Nevertheless, it should be clear that pollution is an issue which affects all of us. Many of the problems described are getting worse and in some instances it may be too late to prevent serious damage. There are those who would say that pollution is the price we have to pay for progress and that part of the environment must be sacrificed if we are to enjoy a satisfactory standard of living. However, if vital natural systems are wrecked by pollution which could be avoided; if children have their brains damaged by lead for the convenience of industry; if drinking water and food become dangerously contaminated by toxic chemicals – in short, if the planet becomes progressively and permanently polluted, this price may be too high to bear.

CZECH CONROY

6 Energy: We can do better than nuclear power

IN ORDER TO assess how important a role nuclear power or any other energy technology can play in British energy policy we have to decide first of all on our objectives. In my opinion there are four key problems that have to be addressed. The following three of these were highlighted by the OPEC price rises in 1973 and 1979:

1. The heavy dependence of virtually all the industrialised countries on imported oil had led to serious security-of-supply problems.
2. The oil crisis reinforced concern about the finite nature of fossil fuels.
3. It showed the harmful impact which energy price rises could have on the whole economy because of the profligate way in which energy was being used in every sector.

Let's examine these problems in detail.

The UK is better endowed with fossil fuels than most countries, with around 300 years' reserves of coal at current rates of consumption, and important reserves of oil in the North Sea. Nevertheless, if primary energy consumption were to grow as projected by the

Department of Energy in 1979, with oil and gas retaining the same percentage shares of the total, the entire reserves (proven and likely) of oil and natural gas over the UK continental shelf would be exhausted within 30 years. Thus, our current energy self-sufficiency would be short-lived, and we would soon be faced with the problem of major fuel imports once again as our domestic reserves of oil and gas ran out.

Before fossil fuel (and uranium) reserves are exhausted, however, increases in the price of fuels are liable to lead to serious macro-economic problems. Until 1973, energy had had little effect on the cost structure of industrialised economies. Thereafter, however, energy price rises had a major effect on inflation, and US studies have shown that the energy crisis was also largely responsible for the poor investment and productivity results over the period 1973–78. Further real increases in oil prices are expected over the next two decades and beyond. The Department of Energy's projections in its Sizewell Inquiry evidence suggest that oil prices could double from the 1980 level of US$30.8 billion by the year 2000. The harmful effects of oil price increases have been succinctly summarised by two US policy analysts as follows:

> Any price increase has immediate, undesirable effects on all oil-importing nations, causing a direct loss in national income. If the price rise is very gradual over a period of many years, thereby allowing the oil-importing nations a gradual adjustment, then the direct effects might be the main ones.
>
> A large, sudden increase in oil prices would have serious indirect effects. It would exacerbate inflation, place further strains on the international monetary system, and sharply contract the demand for goods and services, further reducing national income. In short, the economic consequences would likely be a major recession, or possibly even a depression.

The prices of other finite fuels (gas, coal and uranium) are also expected to increase in real terms over the next two or three decades, partly because of a gradual shift towards less favourable reserves as the least cost ones are exhausted. Increases in the price of energy from these fuels would also have adverse effects on national economies.

Thus, the oil crisis pointed to three priorities for energy policies to address:

- the security of energy supplies,
- the finite nature of fossil fuels, and
- further increases in energy prices.

In addition to these three problem areas there is a fourth one which energy policy must address, namely:

- the environmental hazards of energy consumption.

The main environmental hazards arising from the consumption of finite fuels are acid rain from sulphur dioxide and nitrogen oxide emissions; the build-up of carbon dioxide in the atmosphere; and the possible release of toxic radioactive materials from uranium mines, nuclear reactors and nuclear wastes. Acid rain has given rise to growing concern during the last year or two as the full extent of its effects has become apparent. The biggest threat is from sulphuric acid formed from the sulphur dioxide that is emitted by coal-burning and oil-fired power stations, furnaces and refineries. But oxides of nitrogen released in both power stations and vehicle exhausts are also giving rise to concern, in relation to both acidification, and ozone damage to trees. Acid rain is causing the death of fish and trees, and reducing crop yields and timber production, in many European countries; and some people believe that the damage may be irreversible.

Atmospheric pollution by carbon dioxide is a problem of global significance. In the words of the Council of Environmental Quality, an agency of the US Government:

> Many scientists now believe that, if global fossil fuel use grows rapidly in the decades ahead, the accompanying CO_2 increases will lead to profound and long-term alteration of the earth's climate. These climatic changes, in turn, could have far-reaching adverse consequences, affecting our ability to feed a hungry and increasingly crowded world, the habitability of coastal areas and cities, and the preservation of natural areas as we know them today.

Nuclear power poses another set of environmental risks, starting with the mining of uranium and finishing with the disposal of nuclear wastes. Large quantities of radioactive materials accumulate in the core of a reactor, equivalent to fallout from hundreds of Hiroshima bombs, making it imperative to contain the radioactivity in the event of an accident. Official safety studies, however, have been seriously deficient, and we do not know enough about nuclear reactors to be confident of their safety, as events like the Three Mile Island accident should continually remind us. One particularly toxic material produced in nuclear reactors is plutonium: this, combined with the fact that plutonium can be used as an explosive in nuclear weapons, makes it perhaps the most dangerous element in the world. These factors led the Royal Commission on Environmental Pollution to conclude that:

> . . . [we] should not rely for energy supply on a process that produces such a hazardous substance as plutonium unless there is no reasonable alternative. (Royal Commission on Environmental Pollution 1976)

The Official Response – Nuclear and Coal Extravaganza

The Department of Energy's policy is officially described as a three-pronged one based on coal, conservation and nuclear power, and is known as 'COCONUKE' for short. In reality, however, the policy is almost entirely supply-orientated, with only lip-service being paid to energy conservation. The energy conservation budget has been substantially reduced in recent years (from what was already a relatively low level), and this is widely seen to reflect the Government's fundamental disinterest in conservation. To bring about energy conservation the Government relies almost entirely on increases in energy prices. This policy mechanism has been seriously inadequate, however, because there are major barriers to the working of the market for conservation products which severely limit the efficacy of a policy based on economic pricing.

The main focus of the official strategy is the substitution of nuclear power for oil and gas. It is based on the assumption that electricity will become an increasingly important vector for distributing energy, and that more and more of this electricity will be supplied by nuclear power stations. Ironically, this official strategy is not capable of having a major impact on the four major problems described above.

The Department of Energy's projected contributions of nuclear power and coal would not improve security of supply significantly since their impact on the most insecure fuel, imported oil, would only be marginal. They could gradually displace the use of oil in the public supply of electricity, but this currently represents only about 7.5% of UK oil consumption. This is the only use of oil which nuclear power can directly displace, since in practice it is only capable of producing electricity. Coal can replace oil in some other applications; but neither coal nor nuclear power contributes to road transport, the largest single use of oil (36.5%) at present. (The Department assumes that electrically-driven vehicles will not make a significant contribution to energy demand.) Thus, oil consumption could increase from 110.8 mtce (million tonnes coal equivalent) (1981) to as much as 135.4 mtce in the year 2000.

The Department of Energy's 1979 energy projections showed that net oil imports in 2000 could be running at 35–40 million tonnes of oil per annum. They assumed higher rates of growth in GDP than the latest projections do, so the problem has now been postponed slightly. The latest ones give no indication of oil import requirements: nevertheless, it seems likely that they would entail Britain being exposed to the vicissitudes of an oil-starved world around the turn of the century. Furthermore, large centralized power stations, particularly nuclear stations, have their own security of supply problems, being vulnerable to strikes, sabotage and accidents. Nuclear power also requires imports of uranium, and these could become insecure under certain circumstances.

The increasing emphasis on power stations which produce only electricity inevitably means that fuels will continue to be consumed profligately. The electricity generating boards already consume one-third of the UK's total primary fuel, and convert it into electricity with an average conversion efficiency of only 30% – a very inefficient process. Thus, every year 20% of the UK's primary energy is wasted in reject heat from power stations. A greater proportion of electricity in the UK's fuel mix, therefore, would mean the more rapid depletion of finite fossil fuel reserves rather than their conservation – a policy sometimes described as one of 'strength through exhaustion'.

Nor will nuclear (or coal-fired) stations provide 'low cost' energy as their proponents claim. Although nuclear electricity was once characterised by the media as 'too cheap to meter' it has never been economic in the UK. The capital costs of nuclear stations (the main component of nuclear electricity costs) have been increasing rapidly in real terms both for the UK's advanced gas-cooled reactor and for the world's dominant reactor system, the pressurised water reactor, largely as a result of more stringent safety requirements. A nuclear programme, starting with the PWR which the Central Electricity Generating Board wants to build at Sizewell in Suffolk, would not, therefore, be a sensible economic investment. The Monopolies Commission concluded that electricity costs in England

and Wales would continue to rise in real terms until the late 1990s, and attributed '. . . a substantial element of the increased costs up to that time . . . to the capital charges of the investment programme itself'. Electricity is already a relatively expensive fuel, and it can be expected to remain so if there is a large nuclear programme. Neither domestic coal prices nor coal station costs are likely to rise as rapidly as nuclear station costs, but coal prices are generally expected to increase in real terms between now and the year 2000. The increasing use of electricity envisaged by official policy, with its inefficiency in energy terms, is likely therefore to lead to higher fuel bills for consumers rather than lower ones.

Finally, the official COCONUKE policy makes no attempt to relieve the problems of environmental pollution. Total primary energy demand is projected to be in the range 327.2–549.4 million tonnes of coal equivalent (mtce) in 2010, compared with 344.7 mtce in 1980. In almost all the energy projections, therefore, the environmental problems of acid rain, carbon dioxide pollution, reactor safety, nuclear wastes, etc., would be seriously exacerbated.

The fact that the Government's policy of nuclear expansion does not make sense when assessed against energy policy objectives should not come as a big surprise. Policies tend to be based primarily on political considerations rather than rational argument, and these two factors frequently produce conflicting conclusions.

Originally, nuclear power station orders were based on the 'energy gap' argument – that there would be a shortfall of energy supplies since the official projections showed energy demand greatly exceeding energy supplies before the turn of the century. That argument has now had to be abandoned by the nuclear proponents since energy demand has obstinately refused to increase during the last decade. Instead, the Central Electricity Generating Board's case for building the Sizewell 'B' nuclear station rests upon the argument that it will produce electricity more cheaply than the Board's existing fossil-fuel-fired stations, and that it is therefore worth building the station 'ahead of need'. However, this argument is also losing credibility, and, realising this, ministers have already started saying that even if Sizewell 'B' does not look like reducing electricity prices it would still be worthwhile as a means of diversifying the CEGB's sources of electricity (i.e. substituting nuclear power for coal). When Nigel Lawson was Energy Minister, in March 1983, he said in a speech that this argument for nuclear stations was 'unassailable' – which left objectors at the Sizewell Inquiry wondering why they were bothering to give evidence against this latest argument from the nuclear lobby.

The present Government's enthusiasm for nuclear power has more to do with keeping big business interests happy, and a gut reaction against the miners, than detailed analysis of what kind of energy policy would best serve the national interest. Nevertheless, soundly argued alternatives to the official policy do exist, and serve to highlight the hollowness of the Government's position.

Energy Policy – A New Approach

The transparent inability of conventional policies, with their heavy reliance on nuclear power, to ameliorate the energy problems facing us has stimulated the evolution of a radically different kind of energy strategy. This new kind of strategy has been developed primarily by researchers based in academic institutions and environmental groups in a large number of industrialised countries: in the UK the lead groups have been Friends of the Earth, the International Institute for Environment and Development (IIED) and the Open University's Energy Research Group. The starting point of this alternative approach – variously known as 'soft energy paths', 'low energy futures/strategies', and 'energy-efficient futures' – is a detailed analysis of the nature of the country's energy demand; and it has revealed some surprising facts (see Table I). It shows, for example:

Table I **Energy end uses**

		End use energy
Heat		
< 100°C	55%	
100°–600°C	6%	66%
> 600°C	5%	
Liquid fuels		26%
Essential electricity		8%
		100%

● that two-thirds of the energy delivered to customers is used to provide *heat*, and that most of this heat is required for space and water heating or industrial processes at temperatures below the boiling point of water;

● that one-quarter of delivered energy is required as *liquid fuels* for use in transport;

● that electricity, which occupies such a prominent position in government thinking, is essential for less than 10% of end-uses; and

● that 60% of the energy value of fuels is lost in their conversion to premium sources of energy, and in their subsequent distribution and use.

This new fine-grained approach to energy policy reveals different roles for a multiplicity of energy sources that are largely ignored in conventional policy, and discourages the idea of a single source as a panacea. It is characterised by:

● greater emphasis upon increasing energy efficiency than on increasing energy supply;

● the closer matching of energy sources to actual end-use needs; and

● the substitution of 'natural' or 'renewable' energy sources for finite fuels.

The primary objectives to be achieved by energy strategy are clearly recognised as the provision of adequate and secure supplies of heat and liquid fuels at minimum environmental and economic cost. The basic nature of a soft energy path for the United Kingdom is described below, drawing heavily on work done by Earth Resources Research and IIED.

Improving Energy Efficiency

There is massive scope for improving energy efficiency. A major study by Gerald Leach and his colleagues at the International Institute for Environment and Development concluded that a series of simple, known technical fixes could keep energy (and electricity) demand more or less constant from here on to 2025 while gross domestic product roughly trebles – a three-fold increase in energy efficiency. The study by Earth Resources Research shows that more radical energy efficiency measures than those assumed by Leach *et al.* could bring about a five-fold increase in efficiency over the same period, assuming virtually the same rate of growth in GDP. Substantial efficiency improvements are possible in all sectors of the economy and some of them are described below.

Buildings

A report by the Select Committee on Energy, on energy conservation in buildings, concluded that there are many conservation measures which are '. . . much more cost-effective than most energy supply investment'. The lower cost of energy efficiency measures in buildings has already led many energy utilities in the US to invest (through loans or grants to customers) in such measures in preference to new supply capacity. The Tennessee Valley Authority, for example, has a loft insulation programme which saves electrical energy at less than one-fifth the cost of providing new generating capacity.

Estimates of the scope for cost-effective measures vary according to the definition of cost-effectiveness which is being used. The Building Research Establishment bases its estimates on those measures which are cost-effective at current energy prices, and concludes that they could reduce energy consumption in buildings by 30%; the Property Services Agency has already achieved average savings of 35% in government property using measures cost-effective at current prices. Leach and his colleagues assume that in the medium term, as energy prices rise, cost-effective measures would produce savings of 30–50% in the commercial and institutional sector. The Earth Resources Research study defines an efficiency improvement as cost-effective if the marginal cost to the nation of saving energy is equal to or less than the marginal cost of supply. Using this definition, the study estimates that cost-effective efficiency measures would reduce energy consumption in buildings by about 80%. This is the appropriate definition for assessing the cost-effectiveness of energy investments from the perspective of national energy policy: unfortunately, governments seldom make such symmetrical comparisons between new supply and new conservation investment options.

All of the above calculations are concerned with measures to reduce space and water heating in *existing* buildings. In new buildings efficiency improvements are generally even more cost-effective, and recently constructed buildings in some countries are so energy-efficient that they do not need a fossil fuel or electric heating system; the heat from the occupants' bodies, the appliances (e.g. cooker and lights) and the solar energy entering the fabric of the building is sufficient to keep the building warm.

Apart from space and water heating, energy is used in buildings to run appliances and lighting. There is equally large potential for reducing the energy consumed by electrical appliances and lighting. For example, it has been estimated that straightforward technical improvements can increase the efficiency of lights and appliances in a typical Danish household by a factor of four overall; and that such improvements are highly cost-effective with payback times generally less than two years. Commercially-available household electrical appliances and lamps are steadily increasing in efficiency. Some new Japanese refrigerators are more than twice as efficient as the average 1975 model. The manufacturing companies Philips and Thorn have both produced highly efficient light bulbs, the SL★ series and 2-D respectively. Philips have calculated that their SL★ bulbs, although more expensive to buy than ordinary filament bulbs, can halve the cost of lighting because they are four times as efficient as ordinary bulbs and last about five times as long.

Overall, the efficiency with which energy is used in buildings can be increased by about 30–50% in the medium term with measures which are cost-effective; and by 80% or more in the longer term, particularly as new buildings and new household appliances replace existing ones.

Transport

Road vehicles – mainly cars – account for the vast majority of energy consumed in the transport sector. The efficiency of road vehicles can be improved in a variety of ways, including lighter and more stream-lined body work; smaller engines with significantly reduced internal friction; continuously variable transmission; substitution of diesel for petrol engines; and electronic controls on ignition and carburation. Overall, the average efficiency of the car fleet could be double the mid-1970s average by the turn of the century (i.e. a 100% improvement in efficiency). (The Department of Energy's 1982 energy demand scenarios assume a 33% improvement in the average efficiency of cars by the year 2000, and a 50% improvement – from 30 mpg to 45 mpg – by 2010.) In aircraft, fuel savings of 45% (over the mid-1970s average) are likely by 1990, and savings of up to 60% are possible by 2000.

Industry

The industrial sector is an extremely heterogeneous one, so that the scope for efficiency improvements, and the nature of them, varies considerably. Nevertheless, generally speaking Leach and his colleagues estimated that fuel consumption per pound sterling of output could fall by 22–35% over the period 1976–2010, depending on the sector. Another study concluded, after examining three British factories, that in the engineering sector savings of about 50 per cent are probably cost-effective today. The nature of the energy savings in each of the three factories is shown in Table II.

Table II   **A comparison of the energy saving potential on three engineering sites** (Energy in specified operations is expressed as a percentage of the sum of thermal equivalent of electricity and fuel. Saving is expressed as a percentage of original consumption for that operation.)

Site	Space heat	Saving	Process heat	Saving	Lighting	Saving	Machine tools	Saving	Total	Saving overall
A	63	95	13	0	4	50	15	20	100	67
B	37	95	23	20	3	47	36	17	100	45
C	82	65	1	0	5	30	6	8	100	55

A = Light engineering, B = Aluminium extrusion, C = Heavy engineering.

The two studies summarised above suggest industrial energy consumption per unit value of output could be reduced by 22–50% over the next three decades. With further increases in energy prices, and the gradual replacement of the existing industrial infrastructure, energy consumption in industry could be reduced by 70–80% by 2025.

Implementation

There are many institutional and economic barriers hindering the implementation of energy efficiency measures which are cost-effective to the nation now, or are likely to be so in the near future. For example, householders and small businesses with limited resources have to borrow money at high commercial rates of interest. Consequently, householders often do not invest in energy efficiency measures like cavity wall or loft insulation, even though it would pay them to do so; and small businesses require quick payback times on their investment, often less than two years. By contrast, the nationalised energy supply industries (electricity, coal and gas) can obtain capital from government institutions or banks at lower interest rates; and, applying laxer criteria, they invest in energy supply projects (such as Sizewell 'B') which are far less economically attractive than most energy efficiency investments. These and other barriers to conservation measures are currently leading to a huge misallocation of financial resources in the energy sector.

Future Sources of Energy

Wastage of energy can be greatly reduced if energy supply systems match as closely as practicable the type of energy needed. With this in mind, therefore, various energy supply systems are described in this section, most of which also harness natural energy flows rather than finite fuels.

Heat supply systems

As explained earlier, the vast majority of heat is required for space and water heating. This is the only form of heat supply considered here, therefore, since space limitations preclude a discussion of all forms in which heat is required. The fact that low grade heat for space and water heating is the major end-use in the UK makes it desirable to introduce heat grids or networks in all urban areas. Initially, the heat would be supplied by fossil fuels (mainly coal), and heat from renewable energy sources would be gradually phased in from around the turn of the century.

Fossil-fired combined heat and power systems. Conventional power stations produce electricity with waste heat as a generally useless by-product. If, instead, fuels were converted into heat, with electricity as a by-product, far more of the energy in the fuels could be put to useful purposes: power stations which produce useful (higher temperature) heat and electricity are called combined heat and power (CHP) stations. The fact that they produce usable heat (for space and water heating) means that CHP stations have a conversion efficiency of up to 85% – more than twice the 30% average efficiency of the UK's conventional power stations.

CHP is a widely-used technology in many other countries. Several European countries are already meeting a large proportion of their space and water heating requirements from CHP systems (private and public) and district heating schemes. District heating schemes, an increasingly large proportion of which incorporate CHP, supply 30–35% of the total heating load in Denmark, 30% in Sweden, 20% in West Germany and 55% in the Soviet Union.

CHP systems are cost-effective against existing fuel prices in many cases. For example, the coal-fired CHP/DH scheme in Odense, Denmark, is estimated to supply heat at roughly one-sixth the cost of electric heating. The UK has not even started to build one major CHP scheme as yet; but in 1982 a Government-commissioned study by

W. S. Atkins & Partners reported favourably on the economics of several possible schemes:

> The studies concluded that all the nine schemes considered are feasible and have a prospect of commercial viability. The schemes could provide heat at 10% below the cheapest alternative whilst showing rates of return about or above 5% per year as required of new investment by nationalised industries.

Renewable sources of heat. District heating could provide heat for as much as one-third of households by the year 2000, and for 80% by 2025 – almost all the UK's urban households. Coal-fired CHP systems would be the main source of heat initially, but after the year 2000 various renewable energy sources could make significant contributions. For this reason the Swedish Energy Commission has recommended that 'district heating networks and local hot water networks are designed so as to permit changeover to solar heating', by using systems with relatively low distribution temperatures ($< 95°C$) and suitably dimensioned radiators. Solar energy for district heating can be provided in two ways: active solar heating systems, using flat plate or vacuum tube collectors, with interseasonal storage systems; and solar ponds, which usually comprise a hole in the ground with an impervious liner and a darkened bottom, filled with concentrated brine.

Several active solar heating systems for groups of dwellings or large buildings are already in operation in Sweden. One hot water store at Studsvik, for example, provides virtually all of the annual space heating for an office block; while another, at Lambohov, supplies over 80% of the space and water heating requirements for an estate of 55 large terraced houses. Swedish researchers expect such heating systems, using water as the heat storage medium, to be competitive with conventional oil-fired systems in the late 1980s, and to supply a large proportion of the energy used in Sweden for space heating. A more recently developed system, using ground storage instead of water, is estimated to be competitive in Sweden now, costing 40% less than oil heating. The UK climate is generally better suited to solar heating than Sweden's, and such systems may well, therefore, be competitive in the UK early in the next century.

Solar ponds can also supply heat throughout the year, with the large thermal mass of the pond providing built-in heat storage. Solar ponds are being intensively investigated in the US. For example, feasibility studies suggest that solar pond district heating could supply the entire low-temperature heat demand of Northampton, Massachusetts. Relatively little work has been done on the economics and performance of solar ponds in the UK; but that which has been done suggests that they could make an important contribution to our heat supplies. An official report published in 1976 concluded that 'predicted energy costs seem low enough to justify a closer evaluation of the solar pond concept to small district heating systems in this country'. Work carried out at Sussex University has since confirmed the potentially favourable economics of district heating systems using solar ponds in the UK, and a programme of development and demonstration is underway.

Another natural source of heat that is particularly attractive economically is geothermal energy from hot aquifers. Geothermal district heating schemes are already well-established in several countries. Schemes in France supply heat more cheaply than oil-fired systems, and the French Government has set a target of half a million geothermally heated homes by 1990 with four or five new schemes being commissioned every year. Geothermal heating also has large potential and favourable economics in the UK, but so far only one scheme (in Southampton) is going ahead here. About one-fifth of the UK population lives in areas potentially suitable for geothermal heating; and it is officially estimated that geothermal heat could substitute competitively for coal and would be significantly cheaper than oil or gas on either a group or individual building basis.

Buildings not connected to CHP/DH schemes could obtain their space heating from passive solar systems and water heating from solar panels. A study carried out by the Martin Centre in Cambridge showed that passive solar systems have a large potential application in existing dwellings, with retrofitting of conservatories being appropriate for 44% of houses in Cambridge and perhaps 39% throughout the UK. This national estimate is somewhat higher than that of 15–20% in a previous study, but whatever the correct figure, the potential for passive solar retrofitting is very large. New buildings can be designed so that passive solar gains (and free heat gains from bodies and appliances) are sufficient to keep the building warm throughout the year. The annexe to St George's School in Wallasey is one such building, and has been in use for over 20 years. Houses heated entirely by passive solar gains (and possibly a small amount of heat from their solar water collectors) are now being built in many countries. Even in the relatively cold climate of Saskatchewan in Canada such houses are being built in large numbers on a commercial basis.

Solar water heating systems have been in commercial use in various countries since the end of the nineteenth century. About 4–5 million are currently in use in sunny countries such as Japan, Israel and the United States, but their potential is not limited to sunny climates and production is rapidly increasing in Canada and France. At present only about 20,000 are in use in the UK. Over the next few years, however, improvements like the use of vacuum tube rather than flat plate collectors, and packaged systems (such as that marketed by the Dutch company, EBS) could make solar water heating cost-effective in a large proportion of the UK's existing buildings.

Liquid fuels

Biomass fuels (methanol and ethanol) supplied almost one-fifth of Western Europe's transport fuels (i.e. for a few million vehicles) immediately prior to World War II, and other European countries are planning important contributions from them once more. For example, France is aiming to reduce its dependence on oil for transport purposes by 25–50% over the next 10 years by substituting alcohol fuels, particularly methanol from vegetable sources.

Table III   **Biomass fuel for road transport**

Resource	Quantity available early next century (PJ/yr)	Fraction collected (%)	Conversion efficiency (%)	Methanol produced (PJ/yr)
Refuse	640–840	75	50	240–315
Crop residues	80–100	50	50	20–25
Wood residue	50–50	50	50	10–15
Wood crop	80–50	90	50	35–70
			Total	305–425

(figures rounded)

Alcohol fuels from biomass could also supply a large proportion of liquid fuels for transport in the UK. If the total road mileage remained constant and average vehicle efficiencies improved by 50% for cars and 25% for other road vehicles (see section on improving energy efficiency on pages 100–103), total demand for liquid fuels would be 620 PJ/year or 14 million tonnes of oil equivalent. About 300–400 PJ of methanol could be produced annually in the UK (see Table III), primarily from refuse, meeting 50–65% of the possible delivered energy requirements of a more efficient road vehicle fleet.

Electricity

In an energy-efficient future, demand for electricity would decline as electricity was used more efficiently for essential purposes and phased out for non-essential purposes such as space heating. The reduced level of electricity generation would be supplied by coal-fired CHP stations, wind power and other renewable energy systems.

Wind power is likely to be the major source of electricity from natural energy flows. Estimates of the total technically available wind energy resource, including shallow offshore waters, range from 100 to 350 TWh/year. (At 240 TWh/year, current UK annual electricity demand lies roughly in the middle of this range.) Whatever the actual figure, however, everyone agrees that the resource is large. Furthermore, it is now clear that a substantial wind capacity, perhaps 20–25% of total generating capacity, could be accommodated on the CEGB's grid without major technical difficulties, and that dispersed arrays of wind generators could provide some firm capacity.

Several commercially available medium-sized wind turbines (rated at 50–100 KW) produce electric power at a cost comparable to the corresponding fuel used at a large fossil-fired power station, when evaluated over the lifetime of the plant. The economics of using large (> 100 KW) wind turbines to generate electricity for grid distribution are also looking increasingly attractive, and wind power could, therefore, be making a useful contribution to electricity supplies around the turn of the century.

There are a variety of other technologies for producing electricity from natural energy flows. These include hydro schemes, tidal barrages, photovoltaic cells, and in the longer term wave power and geothermal energy from hot rocks. It is not possible at this stage to say exactly what contribution each technology will make to UK electricity supplies. Geothermal energy from hot rocks, for example, could in principle supply the UK's total energy needs several times over, but it is still at a very early stage of development and it may be that only a small fraction of its potential will be realised. Generally speaking, however, rapid progress is being made in reducing the costs of these systems and most of them look very promising.

International Dimensions

The energy strategy outlined above is related specifically to the UK. Similar analyses have been done in other industrialised countries; however, these analyses have found that the end-use structure of energy consumption is quite similar in virtually all industrialised countries, and that the best strategy for satisfying end-use needs is therefore also quite similar. Preliminary studies for a large number of industrialised countries suggest that the primary energy demand in industrialised countries (East and West) could be reduced to about 60% of its present level while the material standard of living of those countries roughly doubles. Thus, the impact of an energy-efficient future in the UK on the four problems described earlier could be seen as a microcosm of the impact which energy-efficient futures might have at the global level. This is important since some problems, such as carbon dioxide build-up in the atmosphere, require a global solution.

Conclusions

The Department of Energy's demand projections suggest that, assuming a 2.5% per annum growth in GDP, primary energy consumption would be about 430–460 mtce in the year 2000 and would continue rising thereafter (512–549 mtce in 2010). By contrast, the IIED and ERR scenarios, which assume a higher rate of GDP growth (2.9% pa) and therefore a trebling of GDP by 2025, result in primary energy consumption of 361 mtce and 252 mtce respectively in the year 2000. Also by contrast, demand in these scenarios declines substantially between the years 2000 and 2025, by about 25% in the IIED scenario and by 26% in the ERR scenario. (This is due to reduced growth in, for example, traffic levels and the number of households; and the long lead times for some major energy saving technologies).

   The more efficient use of fuels in the IIED and ERR scenarios produces some important benefits for the nation. First, domestic reserves of fossil fuels last much longer. The IIED scenario would enable the UK to remain self-sufficient in oil and gas until almost 2025; and the ERR scenario would result in North Sea oil lasting to 2050 or beyond, and natural gas until about 2100. Coal consumption increases slightly in the IIED scenario and falls dramatically in the ERR scenario, to less than half the current level of consumption by 2025; domestic coal reserves, therefore, would last for at least 250 years and possibly a lot longer in these scenarios. Thus, these energy-efficient futures would virtually eliminate any reliance on foreign fuels until 2025 or beyond, and provide much greater security for the national economy.

A second major benefit of these low energy futures is that they are low energy expenditure futures. They reduce fuel bills by reducing the amount of energy required to perform a given task; and this reduced level of energy consumption leads in turn to a slower rate of increase in energy prices. It is not possible to quantify the benefit of reduced energy expenditure, but in qualitative terms it would mean greater national wealth, reduced inflation and a generally more buoyant economy. Conversely, if the UK does not implement a low energy strategy, and other countries do, our economic problems could be seriously aggravated. The UK will not be insulated from world trade (unless protectionist policies return with a vengeance), and UK manufacturers will be competing with their foreign counterparts. Since most industrialised countries are less well-endowed with fossil fuels than the UK, they are are liable to increase their energy efficiency much more rapidly and produce energy-efficient products (cars, household appliances, etc) which are more attractive to the UK consumer than domestically-produced goods. There are already signs of this happening as other countries, like Japan, take rapid steps to reduce their dependence on oil.

Last, but not least, an energy-efficient future would minimise the environmental impacts of energy usage. Coal and oil consumption would decline, thereby reducing the amount of acid rain and CO_2 pollution; whereas in the official projections consumption increases to about 250–300 mtce by the year 2010. Oil consumption would be phased out in power stations; and would be much reduced in road vehicles in the short term and gradually replaced by clean alcohol fuels in the longer term. Sulphur dioxide and nitrogen oxides pollution from coal use in industry would be minimised by the use of fluidised bed combustion systems, and the overall level of coal consumption would be accompanied by a lower rate of carbon dioxide release to the atmosphere. The US Government's Council on Environmental Quality believes that in tackling the CO_2 problem 'top priority should be given to increasing energy conservation and the use of solar and other renewable energy sources'.

In conclusion, the reasons for pursuing this new approach to energy strategy, instead of the official approach of expanding nuclear and coal supplies, have been clearly summarised by Gerald Leach as follows:

An energy future of this kind is a future of low risk. It offers material prosperity and the benefit of national self-confidence, yet without the nagging conflict-prone pressures of resource constraints and the need for the public to accept large expansions in energy supplies. It would relieve many environmental problems and release for other purposes investments that would otherwise have to go to energy supply.

Further Reading

Cannell, W. and Chudleigh, R. 1983, *The PWR Decision: How Not to Buy a Nuclear Reactor*, Friends of the Earth, London.

Conroy, C. 1982, 'Why Britain Does Not Need a PWR', *New Scientist*, 95, 491–494.

Conroy, C. 1983, *The Economic Case For Not Ordering Sizewell B, Sizewell B Inquiry Proof of Evidence (P7) for the Council for the Protection of Rural England*, Council for the Protection of Rural England, London.

Conroy, C., Flood M. and Gordon, D. 1982, *Eclipse of the Sun? The Future of Renewable Energy Research in Britain*, Friends of the Earth, London.

Department of Energy 1982, *Proof of Evidence for the Sizewell 'B' Public Inquiry*, Department of Energy, London, p. 50.

Flood, M. 1980, *The Big Risk*, Friends of the Earth, London, p. 30.

Flood, M. 1983, *Solar Prospects: The Potential for Renewable Energy*, Wildwood House, London.

Flood, M., Chudleigh, R. and Conroy, C. 1981, *The Pressurised Water Reactor: A Critique of the Government's Nuclear Power Programme*, Friends of the Earth, London, p. 71.

Komanoff, C. 1983, *Capital Costs, Construction Times and Operating Performance of Westinghouse PWRs, Sizewell B Inquiry Proof of Evidence (P1) for the Council for the Protection of Rural England*, Council for the Protection of Rural England, London.

Leach, G. et al. 1979, *A Low Energy Strategy for the United Kingdom*, International Institute for Environment and Development and Science Reviews Ltd, London, p. 259.

Lovins, A. 1977, *Soft Energy Paths: Toward a Durable Peace*, Penguin, Harmondsworth, p. 231.

Monopolies and Mergers Commission 1981, *Central Electricity Generating Board: A Report on the Operation by the Board of its System for the Generation and Supply of Electricity in Bulk*, HMSO, London, p. 360.

Olivier, D. et al. 1983, *Energy-Efficient Futures: Opening the Solar Option*, Earth Resources Research, London, p. 340.

Patterson, W. 1983, *Nuclear Power*, Penguin Books, London.

Royal Commission on Environmental Pollution 1976. *Nuclear Power and the Environment*, HMSO, London, p. 237.

Select Committee on Energy 1982, *Energy Conservation in Buildings, Volume I: Report and Minutes of Proceedings*, HMSO, London, p. 49.

Select Committee on Energy 1983, *Combined Heat and Power, Volume I: Report and Minutes of Proceedings*, HMSO, London, p. 49.

MICK HAMER

7 Transport: Why we have to control the car

TODAY ABOUT 16 people will die in traffic pile-ups in Britain. This tragedy will be largely unreported. The reason is simple: the event is so commonplace that it is not news. The odds are that someone, somewhere in Britain, will die in a road accident before you put this book down.

In addition some 78,000 people every year are maimed and mauled by the vehicles that use our roads. Most of them will bear the scars for the rest of their lives. This is what in the 1930s was called the 'toll of the road', then considered a scandal. It is now, despite road safety policies, accepted as part of the British way of life – the price we pay for 'progress'.

Road transport has a considerable effect on our daily lives, apart from ending some of them. It causes pollution, noise, corrodes our city streets, leads to new roads cutting swathes through our countryside; and for those faced with declining mobility, it creates the prospect of virtual house arrest. Indeed, the automobile, as John Ketas wrote, 'changed our dress, manners, social customs, vacation habits, the shape of our cities, consumer purchasing patterns, common taste and positions in intercourse'.

There are now over 15 million cars on the roads of Britain,

three cars for every 10 people and over twice as many as there were 20 years ago in 1963. There are also four million other motor vehicles, from motor cycles to juggernauts.

One important effect of the car has been to cause a decline of public transport. Imagine 10 people who catch a bus on its way to town every morning. If one person buys a car, the bus operator is suddenly faced with a 10% drop in revenue on this particular service. The operator can either withdraw the service or raise the fares. Let's suppose that the fares go up by 10% to bring the bus service back to the same financial balance it was in at the beginning of the story. But the passengers cannot go back to the beginning, for their fares have increased: consequently, they have an added incentive to start saving for a car.

The example is, of course, highly simplified. Nevertheless it illustrates a process known as the 'vicious circle of decline' of public transport. As more people own cars, so the number of passengers using public transport drops. Consequently fares rise, or services are cut. The passenger has to pay more for less.

The railways were the first to suffer. Twenty years ago, the railways provided a national transport system. It was possible to get to almost every town of any size in Britain. In 1963 there were nearly 17,000 miles of railway, but by 1983 over 6,000 had been closed. Even more dramatic is the decline in the number of stations. In 1963 British Rail had 4,200 stations; it now has only 2,400. Most of the railway closures took place in the late 1960s, and by the early 1970s it was the turn of the buses. Between 1971 and 1981 the National Bus Company, the operator running most of the 'lifeline' rural buses, cut its bus mileage by virtually a quarter.

Almost all these cuts took place in rural areas: the village that lost its railway station in the 1960s then suffered the loss of its bus service in the 1970s.

Just as serious as the axing of whole routes has been the pruning of services. Bus routes that had hourly buses as recently as 10 years ago might now have only daily buses or perhaps even less frequent services. Many rural routes have buses on just one day a week. And, because of attempts to squeeze bus operations so that they can be covered by two shifts a day, many places no longer have late night services.

Yet this is only part of the price we have to pay for the car. In our city streets the car is constantly threatening to squeeze other road users out and finally choke other forms of transport and the city. Of the people that go to work in Central London by road, about

40% go by bus, and 60% by car. Yet all these people are carried by 130,000 cars, and just 3,000 buses.

Road transport also has more direct effects on walking and cycling. Just under a third of people killed on the roads are pedestrians and a further 5% are cyclists. More pedestrians die on the roads than car drivers.

It is not just a question of danger: heavy traffic makes it unpleasant and difficult to cross roads. Britain is one of the few countries in Western Europe without a separate green light for pedestrians to cross the road at *most* sets of traffic lights. Pedestrians are expected to dodge the traffic as it turns left or right. The danger is obvious but the traffic engineer appears unable to tolerate any hold-up to traffic.

Road transport gets up our noses, which isn't surprising, since it produces 8 million tonnes annually of carbon monoxide, a lethal poison. And for good measure it also manufactures a further half million tonnes of nitrogen oxides and 400,000 tonnes of hydrocarbons, as well as 7,400 tonnes of lead. Although road transport is not the only source of pollution, it is one of the most serious. Ninety per cent of airborne lead and 90% of carbon monoxide comes from motor vehicles.

Juggernauts are chiefly responsible for traffic noise. It is officially estimated that over two-thirds of the urban population suffer from an unacceptable level of traffic noise, that is, a noise greater than 65 decibels, a level which was fixed by a Government committee as long ago as 1961. Yet when the Government introduced its Land Compensation Act, which gives householders who suffer from excessive traffic noise a grant for double glazing, it raised the noise limit to 68 decibels, a substantial increase (the decibel scale is logarithmic). The reason for this change was that the Government would have had to pay out too much money if the level had remained at 65 decibels.

The rise of the juggernaut has also had its spin-off for other forms of transport. The railways and water transport have lost custom, and so wharves and freight yards have closed, setting up another vicious circle.

The car divides the country into two nations. There are those who own a car, and those who don't; those who can drive, and those who cannot. These divisions run deep. They set neighbours against each other. They divide families. They split the suburbs off from the city.

A few people gain by having an increase in mobility. Most

people lose. The single most important influence that widespread car ownership has had is to increase the divide between those that have and those that have not. Those that have are 'all right Jack'. But those that don't have cars also have to pay for the rest.

On the basis of a total of 15 million cars in the country, the car lobby often argues that 'six out of 10 households have cars'. The implication is that when a household has a car then this vehicle fully satisfies all the travel needs of that household. But that is not true. Firstly, only a limited number of people in that household can drive. Children and teenagers under the driving age limit cannot drive (at least not legally). They are forced to depend on public transport, walking or cycling. As the number of cars on the roads has grown so these members of our society (except when driven) have lost mobility or independence – or both.

Secondly, very few old people have car licences. They grew up in an age before widespread car ownership and never learnt to drive. Most of them never will. Again, they have lost mobility and independence.

And thirdly, even amongst adults, a substantial number of people can't drive. Roughly six out of 10 adults holding a driving licence are men, and frequently women are unable to drive the 'family' car.

This problem is compounded because of geographical differences between households that have cars and those that do not. Rural areas have high car ownership, as do the suburbs on the city fringe and the commuting towns that surround most cities. Typically, these areas are removed from the city centre. They are, by comparison, sparsely populated. They have poor or non-existent public transport, partly because a lot of households have cars.

Yet even in these areas a substantial number of families remain without cars, and more importantly a large number of mainly women, the young, and the old, are restricted. Even if they have a driving licence they cannot drive if the breadwinner has taken the car. These are the prisoners of privilege.

There are also city centre areas were relatively few people have cars. These areas are heavily populated. They have some of the best public transport services in the country – although even these are not as good as they used to be.

The division is between high density areas, which have few cars, and low density areas, which have many cars. And this division holds for all income groups. Although high density areas tend to have a high proportion of poor families, a rich family in a high density inner city area is far less likely to have a car than a similar household in a low density suburb.

However, these inner city areas with few cars have to pay a high price for the ownership of the cars in the suburban fringe. Every morning rush hour a trickle of cars emerges from the far-flung suburbs and sets out for the city. By the time it has reached the city centre it is a tidal wave of traffic. The cars come from their suburban garages and cause traffic jams on the streets lined by the houses of the carless.

This is one of the reasons behind the apparent contradiction between the popularity of cars and traffic. Owning a car is seen as being extremely desirable: yet traffic is extremely unpopular. It is frustrating and dangerous for pedestrians and cyclists. It impairs the efficiency of bus services and causes motorists to fume at their own confection.

The motorist only encounters serious traffic jams in the city centre. There are far too few cars in their local neighbourhood to cause any serious traffic problems. Hence some of the most divisive and controversial road schemes – like the Archway Road widening scheme in North London. The Department of Transport wants to widen this two carriageway road into a three-lane dual carriageway – an urban motorway. The width of the new road is dictated by the number of cars which the DoT reckons will use it. But very few of these cars will be used by the local community. Many will not even come from North London – they will come from Hertfordshire suburbs like Potters Bar.

There is a two-way link between the structure of our towns and cities and transport. Not only do low density suburbs on the edge of cities tend to have poor public transport and a lot of cars, but the growth in the number of cars and new road building actually creates these suburbs.

Before the war, and before many people had cars, there was a house-building boom around the major cities which created semi-detached suburbs. The rule of thumb that developers then used when considering whether a particular piece of land had development potential was whether it was within easy reach of a railway station. Houses had to be within 10 or 20 minutes' walk of a station – say a mile radius. Now, the rise in car ownership has freed developers from the limitations of a pair of feet. Land can be developed which is 10 or 20 minutes' drive from a station – at 30 mph, a radius of 10 miles. (And indeed, outside the south-east where stations still remain important for commuters to London, the existence of a station is often irrelevant.) This tenfold increase in distance has meant a one-hundredfold increase in development area. Before the car, development was restricted to an area of three square miles, the area encompassed by a one mile walk. But now development can take place over an area of 300 square miles – the area within 10 miles of a station or other significant centre.

In the south-east virtually nowhere is outside 20 minutes' drive of a railway, and therefore no land is safe from development.

Only away from the south-east, and chiefly in places like Scotland and Wales, are there places which are too remote for developers, places which are beyond 20 minutes' drive of a reasonable-sized town.

These car-based estates differ radically from the older developments in towns and cities which are based on walking. In areas which are based on walking there are local shops, post offices, pubs, cinemas and restaurants. But in the car-based estates all these facilities tend to be a drive away. Households in these estates even have further to travel to get to the nearest pillar box and telephone booth.

As the number of cars has increased, so the number of shops, schools, hospitals and pubs has declined. The fundamental reason for this change has been that people with cars will travel further. In Norfolk, for example, Watneys achieved a local monopoly in the 1960s after taking over the local breweries. It then closed a large number of village pubs, reckoning that most of its customers would drive to the next village – where, because of the local monopoly, they would find another Watneys pub. By this device the brewery could make a nice profit by realising its assets and yet at the same time retain most of its custom.

The opening of hypermarkets has also had the effect of reducing the number of other shops. At public inquiries into new hyper-markets, the proposers usually justify the development on the basis of the number of people within easy driving distance; they produce maps with isochrones on them (that is, a contour of a five minutes drive, 10 minutes and so on).

Of course, if people choose to shop at a hypermarket then local shops must lose their custom. The process is complex, and the opening of hypermarkets doesn't put corner shops out of business, because the two shops cater for different trades. Instead, what often happens is that a new hypermarket causes the closure of local supermarkets. These closures can take place in towns miles away from the new superstore, and the local supermarkets may well struggle on for months, even years, before admitting defeat. But again the people who lose, and the people who gain, are different. Those who gain are those with cars; the losers are those who live near the old supermarkets and don't have cars.

All too often a hypermarket is opened on the outskirts of a town and the closure of supermarkets takes place in the town, thus contributing to the rundown of inner urban areas.

The split between the car-owners and the non-car-owners is self-reinforcing. People without cars cannot consider moving into areas without good public transport, or local shops. However much they might want to live in a leafy suburb, far removed from the noise and pollution of the city, they simply do not have that choice, unless they learn to drive and acquire a car.

The split between car-owners and non-car-owners is still largely a split between the rich and the poor. Of the richest 10% of households, 90% have cars, while of the poorest 10%, only 10% have a car. The increase in the number of cars has been a process in which the rich have gained at the expense of the poor. It is not just a process in which the rich gain mobility, but one in which the poor have to pay in terms of unsatisfactory public transport, higher fares, pollution and noise.

In road building, this process is institutionalised by something called 'cost-benefit analysis'. Unlike the railways, roads don't make money. Indeed, the toll roads of the 19th century went out of business because they were bankrupted by the railways. So when it wants to build a new road, the Department of Transport justifies spending public money by cost-benefit analysis. Cost-benefit analysis trades off the cost of building a road against the monetary value of the time saved by the motorists who will use the road (plus a few other minor benefits).

According to this system, the road that is the best value for money is the one that benefits the motorist the most for the least cost. This means building the road on the cheapest possible land (except where this advantage would be outweighed by extra civil engineering costs). In rural areas this means that motorways are routed through agricultural land and in urban areas the road goes through the poorest areas: by definition, those in which few people have cars.

It's not as though these problems are the result of us getting our transport on the cheap. Indeed, the cause of our problems is that we are spending so much on it. In 1981, Britain spent nearly £40 billion on inland transport alone (excluding air travel and water freight): that is, over £700 for each man, woman and child in the country. The average household spends 15% of its income on transport, and this proportion is increasing. Over one-tenth of this spending, £4,500 million, comes from the public purse, and is spent on items like the railways and new motorways.

But the cost is not just a question of cash. The country uses over 30 million tonnes of oil a year, over half a tonne for each person. And nearly 60% of Britain's oil use is for transport. Our transport system is fuelled almost entirely by oil. Cars and lorries use, respectively, petrol and diesel. Most trains and boats also use diesel (the only exception being electric trains but this is a small exception, only 22% of the railways' fuel use comes from electricity – which in turn can come from oil). In all, less than 1% of transport fuel use is not oil.

This dependence on oil, which is likely to continue for a considerable period, is one of the most vulnerable points in the transport system. Despite a lot of research effort there is no realistic alternative to the internal combustion engine. Battery-powered cars do exist (and have done for 90 years) but their range is limited to around 50 miles, and they cost 50% more to buy than a conventional car. To make an electric car that would compete with an internal combustion engine there has to be a technical breakthrough in making a high-powered lightweight battery. A petrol substitute can be made from coal, or from alcohol made from plants. Syncrude, as the fuel from coal is called, would be considerably more expensive than petrol and in any case simply tranfers a dependence on one fossil fuel to another. An alcohol fuel is currently being widely used in Brazil, but while this could be important locally, the chief scientist at the Department of the Environment has convincingly shown that the world does not have enough plant life to devote to making fuel for vehicles.

Thus, for the foreseeable future transport will continue to depend on oil. This is all the more serious because of the pattern of development that has grown up around the car. In low density development many journeys, from going to work, school, shopping or even just visiting friends, are too long to be made on foot, and many places are too distant to be reached conveniently by bicycle. Yet at the same time public transport is poor. In these areas people are therefore locked into high fuel consumption and they do not have an easy escape route. This is perhaps the most intractable of our transport problems.

The answer of successive Governments to these problems has

been feeble. Most of their policies have been designed to increase the growth of traffic, and the problems that go with it. The chief of these has been the road building programme. The first motorway was opened in 1959 and by 1981 there were 1,800 miles of motorway. And despite Government claims that the motorway programme is virtually at an end, road building still continues apace.

These roads have made car travel much easier. In many cases journeys by car, even between major cities, are much quicker than the equivalent train journey. The new roads have generated extra traffic and encouraged people to buy cars. Yet at the same time, Governments have been removing the alternatives to the car, closing railways and cutting the subsidies that public transport needs to keep running.

One of the pressures on Government to follow these policies has come from the powerful road lobby. The main constituents of this lobby are the motor industry, the lorry operators and the motoring organisations. Broadly, the road lobby exerts pressure for more roads – the people are voting with their wheels as the RAC puts it – while laying claims to vote for each wheel. The lobby also fights against restrictions on traffic, and demands unfettered movement for the motor vehicle.

The lobby has had some remarkable victories, including the increase in the maximum weight limit of heavy lorries in 1983 from 32.5 tonnes to 38 tonnes. This victory was achieved in the face of considerable environmental opposition and in spite of a large revolt on the Government's own back benches.

Yet perhaps as effective as the road lobby itself has been the pro-road group inside the Department of Transport. The DoT is sometimes accused of 'loading' inquiries into road schemes. The best and hardest evidence, not only of the DoT's pro-road bias but also of its gerrymandering, comes in a memorandum written by one of its top civil servants, Joseph Peeler, who was discussing how to set up an inquiry into raising the maximum weight of heavy lorries. Peeler, who actually used the word 'rigging' in his memorandum, wrote:

> An inquiry offers a way of dealing with the political opposition to a more rational position on lorry weights . . . it should provide a focus for the various road haulage interests to get together, marshall their forces and act cohesively to produce a really good case which should not merely establish the main point at issue but should do good to their now sadly tarnished public image. This would make it easier for the Government to propose legislation . . . in their favour.

The inquiry was eventually set up, despite this leak. It was chaired by Sir Arthur Armitage. It came to the conclusion (surprise, surprise) that lorry weights should be increased. They were.

Twenty years ago, in the era of Beeching and Buchanan, people believed in universal car ownership. But the future isn't what it used to be, and no one believes any more that everyone should have a car. Even in the United States, where more people have cars than anywhere else in the world, one in four households are without cars.

The choice is now between a society built around four wheels, or one which is built around people. The wheeled society is one that cannot ultimately be sustained. The more progress we make towards it, the more difficult will be the breaking of the habit, and the worse will be the withdrawal symptoms.

The alternative is a transport system based on walking or bicycles. Walking is the most universally available form of transport. It is cheap, healthy and immediately accessible. The one important limitation on walking is distance. People will walk half a mile (indeed walking is likely to be quicker over these short distances than any other form of transport); but they cannot be expected to walk five or ten miles.

Walking is therefore only part of the answer. For longer journeys people need buses and trains. The bulk of bus journeys are between two and 10 miles, while train journeys tend to be longer. But in order to use public transport, bus stops and railway stations have to be within easy walking distance.

The alternative therefore involves planning our towns and cities so that the places we live, work and shop in are either easy to walk to, or are well served by public transport.

One of the fundamental changes necessary is to increase the population density of many settlements. The greater the number of people living within a given area, then the more shops, post offices, banks, pubs and public transport that area can support. An increase in density does not necessarily mean tower blocks, overcrowding, or even homes without gardens. The leafy Victorian squares in many inner city areas – like Islington and Kensington in London – have a higher density than the tower blocks of the East End. What it does mean, however, is a greater separation between the town and the country, so that the suburbs are curtailed.

This change is quite easy to achieve practically. In areas where planners want to increase the density they can simply impose a minimum density, below which they will not give planning permission. This is not a radical change. For years the Department of

Environment has operated a maximum population density – a policy which has encouraged suburban sprawl and a decline in the profitability of public transport. And several foreign cities, Hamburg for one, do operate a minimum density requirement. It is one reason why this city can operate a good public transport system without a large subsidy. (If you double the population density within walking distance of a bus stop then you double the number of people who will use that bus.)

However, increasing densities is a long-term policy, which has to be pursued consistently over a long time. Short of knocking down many of our suburbs and other recent low density development and starting anew (which would be expensive and wasteful) densities cannot be changed overnight. But, over a 20 or 30 year period, a major change can be wrought, just as it has been in the last 30 years. The relatively long time it takes to change densities simply underlines the need to plan ahead, and start making a change in our density policy now.

Along with this change two other policies need to be pursued, one designed to provide more local facilities. When these are facilities like hospitals, and provided by the public sector, then this is simply a matter of, in the case of hospitals, health service policy. When they are in the private sector then local authorities can give help by finding suitable premises, assisting with planning permission and giving rate rebates. None of these measures is a radical departure from present practice. Central and local government need to pursue a consistent policy.

The second policy is to support and improve public transport. There is nothing inevitable about the decline of public transport in this country. It is simply a British disease. In most other countries, the use of public transport is increasing. One reason for this is that fares are much lower. British Rail's fares are the highest in Europe, and London Transport's are amongst the highest. Even after the fares reduction in the spring of 1983, the minimum fare in central London at 40p was twice that in Paris: and the Paris fare covers a far larger area than just central London.

The other major change in transport policy is the need to curb the car. Most of the problems of the car are related to their sheer numbers. Individually, a car is no problem; it can even be beautiful, much as any other piece of engineering can be. But in their millions cars are objectionable. One person's car is another person's traffic.

Take road accidents as an example. People die on the roads because we have tons of metal charging around at upwards of 30 miles per hour, banging into other tons of metal and some rather vulnerable people on foot and on bicycles. In urban areas this is an immense and under-rated problem. Over 80% of accidents in which pedestrians are killed occur in urban areas; on the other hand, the bulk of deaths among vehicle occupants are outside urban areas. The explanation for this imbalance is that most vehicle drivers kill themselves at high speeds, high enough to overcome the protection that their metal box gives them, while in urban areas pedestrians die because people have to walk along the same roads that cars use.

One answer, which was tried in the 1960s, was to segregate pedestrians and vehicles, either by putting pedestrians on the walkways, or by sinking them underground in subways. This attempt to force pedestrians to become second-class citizens (by removing them from the streets where they live) failed. People objected to rain- and wind-swept walkways and refused to use smelly (and sometimes dangerous) subways. The other obvious way of segregating the two (by putting vehicles underground) has never really been tried – it is just too expensive, would often require the demolition of buildings and would create tremendous ventilation problems.

The only real answer is to exclude many cars from urban areas, giving the towns and cities back to the people they belong to. This need not be a blanket exclusion. It can be selective, so that cars are only excluded from parts of the town, or for parts of the day or night. The ban can include other vehicles, or not. It can include only some cars, for example those with odd numbered licence plates, one day, even numbered the next. It can be partial exclusion based on licence fee, or it can be operated by selective road narrowings or closures on routes from the suburbs to the city centre.

Different plans will suit different areas. But what will suit all is a target of reducing the volume of traffic. This is the only real hope of cutting accidents and pollution. It will also improve public transport (by cutting delays to buses).

By contrast, the Government's best answer to road accidents is the Green Cross Man. He is paid by the Department of Transport to tour schools, telling the children to look left, right and. . . . The adverts for Renault Fuego enthuse: 'the top of the range Renault Fuego GTX will scorch from 0–60 mph in just 10.1 seconds'. The average toddler takes about twice that time to cross the road.

Further Reading

Bagwell, Philip S. 1974, *The Transport Revolution from 1770,* Batsford.

Hamer, Mick 1974, *Wheels within Wheels – a study of the road lobby,* Friends of the Earth (out of print).

Hamer, Mick 1976, *Getting Nowhere Fast,* Friends of the Earth, (out of print).

The Independent Commission on Transport 1974, *Changing Directions,* Coronet Books.

Lester, Nick and Potter, Stephen 1983 edition, *Vital Travel Statistics,* Transport 2000.

CHRISTINE THOMAS

8 Conservation: Tackling unnecessary waste

'WHEN WILL WE run out of resources?' has been a key question in the environmental debate since the 'Limits to Growth' arguments and projections of the early 1970s. Barbara Ward and René Dubos, in *Only One Earth* (a report produced for the UN Conference on the Human Environment in 1972) wrote that:

> The depletion of natural resources is of course one of the chief reasons of uncertainty concerning the continued ability of the earth to support human civilisations.

This concern with 'how much is there' and 'how long will it last' in relation to our reserve of natural resources, although perhaps dominating the discussion, is not the only reason why we should care about resource conservation. Our increasing consumption of resources, together with the increasing volume of waste this generates, is destroying our natural environment. Mining, quarrying, and disposal of resources all affect environmental quality, and more often than not the effect is detrimental.

We must add to those issues the moral and ethical environmental questions of our society's attitude to resource exploitation. Is a society which consumes and wastes resources on the scale we do today, without consideration of future generations, defensible? A well known American Indian, Chief Seattle, doubted this, and gave the following advice to the 'white man' in his speech of 1854:

> The earth does not belong to man; man belongs to the earth. This we know. All things are connected.
> The earth is not his (white man's) brother, but his enemy and when he has conquered it, he moves on. He kidnaps the earth from his children. His appetite will devour the earth and leave behind only a desert.

Increasingly, too, the connection is being made between the domination and exploitation of nature and natural resources and that of people, whether by sex, colour or wealth. More and more women are making the connection between their own exploitation and the exploitation of the earth. Carolyn Merchant, in *The Death of Nature* and Susan Griffin, in *Women and Nature* both document the historical association of women and nature and the scientific subjugation of both.

Western science has since the 17th century deliberately sought to dominate and control nature, and our technical and industrial society is based on these assumptions; the fundamental relationship in our society is one of domination and exploitation. We need now to develop a society, and a technology, that does not exploit either nature or people; one that is sustainable into the future.

The need for resource conservation is rarely disputed; what is questioned, however, is the extent of conservation required and how to tackle it. Is it sufficient to stem the tide of waste and recycle materials back into the productive system or are further measures required which confront more fundamental aspects of resource use? These may involve reducing waste at source, changing consumption patterns, reusing goods, and designing products for longer life, multiple-use, and repair. Reclaiming and recycling waste materials also have a major role to play in resource conservation. Although not panaceas for the resource and pollution problems created by growing consumption levels, significant environmental benefits would result from greater use of reclaimed materials instead of virgin raw materials; since most recycling processes generate less pollution and require less energy than the production of similar products from virgin raw materials.

Resource Depletion and Environmental Quality

'Experts' often disagree on the geophysical limitations of natural resources. On the basis of a considerable body of knowledge concerned with predicting and analysing data on the availability of resources, some maintain that it is not a question of whether, but when reserves of minerals and fuels will run out. Others argue that this is too simplified a view of the situation, and that as any particular resource becomes scarcer its price rises, resulting in intensified exploration for new reserves and the search for substitute materials. This latter view, that the problems of resource supply will be solved by the price mechanism 'drawing forth' new reserves, obviously depends on new reserves being available, itself a highly debatable issue. It is often argued that as high-grade deposits of resources are exhausted they will be substituted for by deposits of lower-grade ores, their ability to substitute being dependent on there being larger reserves of the lower-grade deposits. This is not necessarily always the case, however: there are real physical limits. We are rapidly reaching the point where there is more metal to be found in rubbish dumps than in some mining deposits.

Also, lower-grade ores usually cost more to extract, particularly in terms of capital investment in plant and equipment, the labour involved and the energy required. With the end of the era of cheap energy, the extra energy required to extract lower-grade ores will make them very expensive to use.

In addition, lower-grade ore deposits generate more wastes, due to the higher proportion of overburden (rocks and soil in which ore is found). These wastes must be disposed of and in doing so a demand for more land is created, and in some areas land itself is becoming an increasingly scarce resource. Scarcity of land may in turn limit the exploitation not only of non-renewable but also of renewable resources. There is already conflict in many parts of the world between forestry and other uses of valuable and scarce land, leading to the destruction of much of our native forests.

Scarcity is not the only factor to consider; the environmental degradation and loss of amenity associated with extracting or harvesting raw materials is also important. Generally in the case of non-renewable resources these effects increase as the resources themselves become less abundant and as poorer-quality ore bodies are exploited with a higher percentage of overburden and hence wastes. The adverse effects of resource exploitation on environmental quality are in many respects as, if not more, serious than resources running out. The effect on environmental quality of any production process or resource-use policy is a wide-ranging and complex matter, involving many interrelated factors. These may include air and water-borne polluting emissions, energy consumption, solid and liquid wastes produced, water-use, noise pollution, visual amenity, and effects on plants and animals.

A resource need not be in short supply to cause adverse environmental effects. Glass is a product whose raw materials (sand, limestone, and soda ash) are abundantly available in Britain, but which cause problems of environmental degradation when they are quarried. Some of the best quality British sands come from the Lower Greensand formation in the King's Lynn and Redhill areas, far removed from the main glass manufacturing centres of Lancashire and Yorkshire. Expanded quarrying of these high-grade sands will involve environmentally sensitive areas where amenity and ecological losses will be great.

Similar environmental impact problems are caused by the extraction of limestone, also used in glass manufacture and found in areas such as the Peak District and the Yorkshire Dales. Due to the high amenity value of these areas, the noise, heavy transport and pollution that would be caused by increased quarrying may not be considered acceptable.

Paper-making consumes vast areas of forest; every year, Britain uses a forest the size of Wales in paper alone, and much of this is thrown away after a brief, useful life. This enormous demand on forest resources can be very disruptive of the ecological balance of forested areas. This is particularly so where, due to expanding demand, wood-pulping operations extend into large areas of presently unexploited forest. To bring a natural, unmanaged forest under management it is sometimes necessary to replace the natural forest vegetation by forest monocultures, plantations of economically profitable trees. Not only are the 'natural', economically useless, trees destroyed, but the loss of habitat and changing conditions may destroy many native species adapted to live in a particular forest environment.

The spread of easily-managed forest monocultures can also lead to soil erosion, and to changes in soil quality and nutrient levels, and may also cause long-term climatic effects.

Resource Conservation

Resource conservation and improvements in environmental quality can be achieved by a variety of changes in the way we use resources, including reducing the quantities of resources used in our society, reducing waste, reusing goods and materials and reclaiming and recycling them. In the absence of any resource policies, priorities in resource conservation at least in Britain have not been established. Neither are the necessary comparisons of the scarcity and the environmental costs of obtaining various resources readily available. Such comparisons should take account of a wide range of factors such as resource scarcity, energy costs, amenity loss, pollution and the generation of wastes, as well as political factors such as the distribution of, and access to, reserves. Priorities for conservation can only be established when this information is available.

Waste is and should be an important factor in any materials-use policy. The Waste Management Advisory Council, a government body, expressed this as follows:

> A comprehensive waste management policy therefore should also aim, within economic and technical constraints, to avoid creating waste and to make the most efficient use of materials at all stages of a product's life.

There are two main ways in which problems of waste can be tackled. Waste can be partly avoided at source by changing product design, marketing practices and consumer attitudes, or it can be reduced after products have been manufactured, through their components being reused, reclaimed and recycled rather than discarded.

A fundamental issue is the desirability of a 'growth' economy involving increased growth in the production of consumer goods which themselves constitute waste in a short time. To tackle resource scarcity it is essential to investigate ways of reducing waste at source. Whilst reclamation and recycling of waste help, they are certainly not absolute solutions. In a situation of increasing raw material consumption (which is that aspired to, if not realised in recent years) reclamation and recycling can only 'buy time' by helping to slow down the depletion of raw material reserves of non-renewable resources. Reducing unnecessary waste of resources, and unnecessary production of consumer goods, is considered desirable because it also reduces the adverse effects on environmental quality caused, in many instances, by their production and consumption.

How can we waste less?

Unnecessary waste of resources can be avoided by changes in the design or distribution of a product, or in consumption patterns. The design of products plays an important role here; particularly in relation to the durability of a product.

Shorter product lifetimes may be encouraged by built-in obsolescence, either as a result of a deliberate policy of the manufacturer to ensure that its products wear out quicker than they might, or because the products are designed in such a way that their repair becomes impossible. Premature obsolescence can also result from a lack of available spare-parts and the inadequate provision of after-sales service.

There are a number of other ways in which design can play an important role in creating or preventing unnecessary waste. Many products can be designed either to be used once and thrown away or for multiple use or reuse; some materials could be substituted by a more abundant or environmentally less damaging resource; and unnecessary waste can result from the overspecification of quality in certain products. For example, often chemically pulped papers are employed where a mechanically-pulped paper of poorer quality could be subsituted. In the production of a similar quality paper, mechanical pulping generally consumes fewer trees, requires less energy and water and generates less pollution than chemical pulping.

However, the design of products is not the only cause of excessive consumption. Consumer attitudes and preferences also play an important role. Overspecification in the design of a product may be the result of proven or imagined consumer preferences and, conversely, consumer preferences may themselves be developed by the advertising and marketing of particular designs. It is, therefore, often difficult to dissociate cause from effect.

This issue has aroused a great deal of interest, particularly in connection with concern about overpackaging. Friends of the Earth drew attention to many of the undesirable aspects (as well as the advantages) of packaging in a report *Packaging in Britain* published in 1973. Since then the debate has continued but little has been resolved. In September 1974 the Government's consultative Green Paper *War on Waste* stated that:

> Packaging does have a particularly short life, and is frequently intended to be discarded as soon as it has been used once. It does therefore involve a rapid using up of the resources contained in it. . . . In the Government's view it is therefore right that greater efforts should be made to avoid the use of wasteful packaging and to devise systems for the economic reuse of containers or the reclamation of the materials they are made of.

That some packaging is excessive seems to have been agreed, but precise definitions of what constitutes wasteful packaging and what should be used to control it are much disputed. Some packaging is obviously necessary, and the primary function of any package should be to contain and protect its contents. However, with the growth of self-service shopping greater packaging has been necessary for control of quantities sold, prolonged shelf-life and information about the product. In addition the importance of packaging in terms of advertising (and hence selling) a product has increased. Impulse buying has been found to be more common in self-service stores than in other retail outlets, and packaging design plays an important role in attracting the consumer's attention. However what is considered useful, even essential for manufacturers and retailers, may not be in consumers' interests, and may be environmentally damaging; where do we draw the line?

Recycling can help too . . .

The approach to reducing waste which has attracted most attention is undoubtedly recycling. Reclaiming and recycling waste materials has been seized upon as an area of activity immediately (or almost immediately) accessible to action, an area where something can actually be done about waste.

Reclamation and recycling are complementary activities. *Reclamation* refers to the process of making a product which has come to be considered as waste *available* for further use; its *processing* for further use is known as recycling. The form which the item will take after being reprocessed may be similar or markedly dissimilar to its original use. Recycling covers a very diverse range of processes, including the repulping of waste paper to make new paper, the use of broken glass in road surfacing, and pyrolysis – a process which converts plastic and organic wastes into liquid and gaseous fuels. Reclamation is generally understood to be a collection, sorting and storage operation, involving only that processing required to assist transportation and handling of the materials. Reclamation and recycling are not always distinguished as separate activities and often described together as either reclamation or recycling activities.

Waste is a human concept; in nature nothing is wasted. Carbon, oxygen, nitrogen, water and many other substances naturally recycle themselves. Each cycle is composed of a number of different steps and overall each cycle can be regarded as a 'closed' system for any particular material, a system in which none of the material is lost. In contrast, however, most industrial processes are 'open' systems. Raw materials are extracted, processed, used and discarded as waste. In recycling we seek to close this loop by returning waste to the processing state; however there are limitations that make 100% recycling of industrial wastes impossible. In particular, growth in consumption, or energy limitations, and even some physical laws, restrict the proportion of materials that can be recycled. The limitations to recycling are often made far worse by the domestic and industrial practices which we have evolved. Industrial processes take a resource from a dispersed state, refine and process it with energy inputs, and thus increase its concentration. The industrial process then proceeds by product design to combine this concentrated material with many other materials, and to distribute the resultant products throughout the country and even the world. By so doing, resources become even more dispersed than they originally were. Combining materials together, particularly in small quantities, makes recycling difficult as it is energy expensive to reverse the process and to recover any one material. Wide distribution networks that have no built-in return system are similarly energy-expensive to correct.

It is important to distinguish clearly between material and energy resources, for while materials can be recycled, energy cannot. Energy is used at every step of every process in the initial manufacture of a product from its raw materials, and further inputs of energy are required later to recycle it into a new product. However, since it is often the case that less energy is needed to manufacture a product from reclaimed rather than raw materials, recycling can result in energy savings.

The benefits of reducing the waste of materials by recycling are obvious. Total quantities of wastes are not affected by recycling programmes, but those we have actually to dispose of can be significantly reduced. Recycling also has the direct effect of reducing demand for a raw material where the waste product is used as a substitute for that raw material, and the more times a material is recycled the more this substitution effect is increased. However, the overall impact of recycling in reducing resource demands will depend on past and future levels of resource consumption. Assuming that there is some growth in the consumption of a resource known to be reaching the limits of its reserves, even maximum reclamation of all available waste material would only serve to postpone shortage of that material for a limited period, complete reclamation (i.e. 100%) being unobtainable. Some of the material used will be too widely dispersed to reclaim: some changed or destroyed in use, such as cigarette papers and lead in petrol; and some in use indefinitely, such as certain books, or steel in bridges.

Recycling not only brings benefits by reducing waste, and achieving some degree of resource conservation; it can contribute to improvements in environmental quality. The recycling of reclaimed materials will in virtually all cases result in substantially less pollution than the processing of virgin raw materials, and will lessen the environmental degradation and loss of amenity associated with raw materials extraction, a point made by the US Environmental Protection Agency:

> Enough is known about the relationships involved to indicate that the net national environmental effects will be beneficial in virtually all instances where resource recovery (reclamation and recycling) is concerned and beneficial almost by definition for source reduction (reduction of waste at source).

The energy requirements for a number of metals produced from secondary materials as compared with products from their ores shows that in the former case energy needs are invariably smaller, often dramatically so. For example the production of copper from US open-pit mined ore can require about 10 times that required for production from municipal scrap; and aluminium, more dramatically, requires about 30 times the energy to be produced from bauxite than when it is recycled from scrap. Steel produced from scrap requires about 30% of the energy of that produced from iron-ore. This energy comparison is likely to become more significant as we seek our new supplies from even lower-grade ores or resource deposits.

Recycling paper also offers considerable potential energy savings. A number of environmental impact analyses have been carried out assessing energy savings achieved by recycling waste paper compared to production from virgin pulp; these typically concluding that a saving in energy of between 50% and 70% is achieved when recycled pulp is used compared to virgin wood pulp.

Recycling glass saves small amounts of energy in melting; a 10% increase in the use of cullet (waste glass) rather than raw materials would give an energy saving of almost 2% in the furnace. The Glass Manufacturers' Federation argue that this represents a small but significant saving. However, more significant energy savings have been claimed for the reuse of containers; in the order of 25–40%.

Energy savings can also be achieved through reclamation and recycling activities in waste management practice. The energy cost of various waste management methods show that landfill (treated or untreated) and non-recuperative incineration make net energy losses per tonne of waste treated; and that reclamation, production of refuse-derived fuel, and incineration with steam raising make net energy gains. The energy balance for local authority waste management practice in 1978/9 was an overall loss of over 1000×10^{12} J. This energy deficit could be turned into an overall energy saving if greater emphasis were placed on reclamation, and on energy recuperation from domestic refuse.

When comparing pollution levels generated by production from reclaimed material with virgin raw materials, the pollutants created by recycling must obviously be considered. In some cases these can cause concern, such as those from secondary-metal smelters and the de-inking of waste paper. However, in most cases, when the complete processes from the acquisition of a material to its disposal are compared, high levels of recycling are found to be associated with lower pollutant discharges.

One exception occurs where a bright, relatively high-quality paper is produced from lower-grade waste, involving significant upgrading during recycling. When de-inked waste paper is used the non-polluting benefits from recycling will be lessened.

Overall, however, it is the wood-pulping process which creates the most pollution in paper making, and when this is taken into account it is found that an increase in recycling will reduce the overall pollution created by paper production, although this reduction will be smaller if unnecessarily high quality standards are maintained.

A reduction in pollution is also associated with other examples of recycling and reuse. Significant savings have been found for returnable glass containers and reuseable plates over their 'throwaway' counterparts. Also substantially lower pollution levels have been found to be associated with the processing of reclaimed steel than in comparison to production from virgin raw materials; a percentage reduction of 76% in water pollution and of 86% in air pollution.

How much do we waste?

It has been estimated that each year in Britain over 170 million tonnes of waste materials are disposed of. Nearly 150 million tonnes of this total are industrial wastes, comprising 110 million tonnes of mining and quarrying waste, 12 million tonnes from power stations, 3 million tonnes from building work, and about 23 million tonnes of general industrial waste. The remaining wastes, just over 25 million tonnes, are in domestic refuse.

Industrial wastes, making up the bulk of waste materials generated annually, are a very diverse group of material ranging from the inert and innocuous to those which present some hazard in disposal due to the toxic, corrosive, combustible, caustic or irritant nature of the material. It is extremely difficult to generalise about the disposal, reclamation or recycling of 'industrial wastes', especially in view of inadequate data about their quantities, composition and potential hazards.

Mining and quarrying wastes form an important group of waste materials. Most of these are relatively innocuous; however, their sheer bulk often creates considerable problems of disposal. These wastes cover a total of between 14,000 and 19,000 hectares of land. Maximising the use of these wastes is the only way to reduce this land dereliction as a result of dumping. Recycling activities generally could contribute to reducing the environmental impact of mining and quarrying in two ways; first by reducing the quantity of waste dumped, and second by reducing the need for raw materials to be mined and quarried. Some industrial wastes are available as homogeneous, concentrated supply of material and are therefore considered as high-grade wastes, easily reclaimed and recycled. Much of this type of material in fact will not even be recorded as an industrial waste material, as it will either be recycled within the plant or has become an industrial by-product, sold for further processing or recycling. The 150 million tonnes of industrial wastes referred to above does not include those wastes already reclaimed and recycled, but refers to those disposed of every year.

The composition of domestic refuse in Britain varies considerably from area to area, and periodically attempts are made to define an average composition for the country as a whole, usually taken from detailed local analyses. One such analysis classified seven groups of waste material in domestic refuse: paper (33%), glass (10%), metals (10%), rag (3.5%), plastics (1.5%), vegetable and putrescible matter (18%) and dust and unclassified waste (24%). A significant percentage (probably around 30%) of these wastes are packaging materials.

Only a very small amount of these wastes (about 1%) is currently reclaimed and recycled; the rest being disposed of, predominantly to landfill (89%) and by incineration (10%). Both these methods are used predominantly to facilitate the disposal of refuse, although some landfill is used as a means of reclaiming derelict land, and a small amount of energy recovery is practised with incineration. Waste utilisation or reclamation is given a very low priority in current solid waste management practice.

The small amount of reclamation carried out by collection authorities involves predominantly the separate collection of waste paper and more recently (due to the introduction of 'Bottle Banks') the separate collection of waste glass. Some paper and metals (non-ferrous and ferrous) are also reclaimed by Waste Disposal Authorities, using hand and mechanical separation of ferrous metals. Other waste utilisation methods currently used include composting and the production of Refuse Derived Fuel (RDF).

Current waste management policies have hardly begun to exploit the resource potential of domestic refuse. Among the domestic and commercial wastes discarded are almost 8 million tonnes of paper, some 2 million tonnes of iron and steel (mostly in the form of 7,500 million tin cans) and 6,500 million glass containers. Domestic refuse also has considerable potential as a fuel source, with, it has been estimated, up to almost 8 million tonnes a year available to be burned as Refuse Derived Fuel, leading to coal savings of up to 3 million tonnes per year. However, its use as fuel does not maximise the value of domestic refuse as a resource. Recycling through source separation and separate collection of wastes produces both greater potential energy savings and other environmental benefits. For example, it has been estimated that the net energy yield achieved by the production of RDF per tonne of waste processed is 4,000 MJ compared with 5,322 MJ saved by sorting and recycling the paper contained in the same tonne of waste.

Nevertheless, recycling activity is far from non-existent in Britain. A large and active industry is responsible for a wide range of reclamation and recycling activities. For paper and metals in particular, British recycling rates compare favourably with those in other EEC countries. For example, the recycling rate (that is, the percentage of total production accounted for by reclaimed material) for iron and steel is over 50%, and for paper about 44%. However, these recycling rates refer to the total amount of waste used in each particular materials industry, including that which arises and is used within the same plant, manufacturing wastes, and post-consumer waste (discarded or used materials). When post-consumer wastes only are considered, our reclamation and recycling performance looks poor indeed. Taking iron and steel again as an example, the recycling rate for post-consumer waste is only about 10%.

Conclusions

In its discussion of the need to conserve raw materials and fuels, the Government's Green Paper *War on Waste*, published in September 1974, expressed a sentiment commonly voiced in recent years:

> The Government believes that there should be a new national effort to conserve and reclaim scarce resources – a war on waste involving all sections of the community. We all instinctively feel that there is something wrong in a society which wastes and discards resources on the scale we do today.

Since then, a clearer picture of the nature and quantity of reclaimable materials and the potential for recycling has emerged: but little else. A picture which shows considerable scope for increasing reclamation and recycling, providing a positive approach is taken clearly recognising the failure of the market to reflect the full social cost of resource use. It is not enough to encourage reclamation and recycling in cases where they are already cost effective. Government initiatives could make these activities economically worthwhile and in view of the direct and indirect benefits available, this should be the aim of policy. Sadly, such policy is lacking.

As well as from government, new initiatives must come from local authorities, industry and individuals. Individuals and voluntary/community groups can play an important part in influencing the climate of opinion towards waste, as well as contributing practically towards waste reduction. This can be done by rejecting wasteful products, by showing a preference for repair and renovation over a new consumption, by instigating local reclamation schemes and by promoting local recycling schemes which could provide the basis for some industry and employment in the community. The development of reclamation and recycling activities has been repeatedly proposed to create and help alleviate high unemployment. This is often combined with a desire to create jobs which benefit rather than destroy our environment.

Reclamation and recycling are a group of activities often referred to in discussion of appropriate or alternative technologies and the development of community industries. Recycling could play an integral role in the development of self-reliant communities, making resources available to the community, bringing it closer to self-reliance. A few small steps, such as those proposed above, could take us towards such a goal rather than letting us drift further towards a world of waste.

Further Reading

Barbier, Edward B. 1981, *Earthworks: Environmental Approaches to Employment Creation*, Friends of the Earth.

Hayes, Denis 1978, *Repairs, Reuse, Recycling – First Steps Toward a Sustainable Society*, Worldwatch Institute, Washington DC.

Porteous, Andrew 1977, *Recycling Resources Refuse*, Longman.

Thomas, Christine 1979, *Material Gains: Reclamation, Recycling and Reuse*, Earth Resources Research Ltd, London.

Vogler, John 1978, *Muck and Brass: A Domestic Waste Reclamation Strategy for Britain*, Oxford Public Affairs Unit, London.

Vogler, John 1981, *Work from Waste: Recycling Wastes to Create Employment*, Intermediate Technology, England.

Some useful journals

Materials Reclamation Weekly (Maclaren Publications Ltd).

Resources Policy (Butterworths; quarterly).

Resources and Conservation (Elsevier Scientific Publication Co; quarterly).

PART 3

● FRIENDS OF THE EARTH

WALT PATTERSON

9 A Decade of Friendship: The first ten years

SOME CALLED THEM Friends of the Earth. Others called them FoE, and meant it. They came into being in California; now the earth has Friends from Tokyo to Nairobi, from Goteborg to Penang. Among its oldest Friends are those in the UK. This is how their Friendship came about.

David Brower was an American mountaineer and writer. A veteran of many environmental battles, he saw the need for a new, aggressive campaigning organization, to tackle environmental issues of every kind. He gathered a circle of like-minded people; and in 1969 they became the first Friends of the Earth. This benevolent name was counterbalanced by its pugnacious acronym – FoE. In 1970 Brower travelled to Europe, met more like-minded people and with them agreed to establish Friends of the Earth in France, Sweden and the UK.

FoE UK was to be 'a company limited by guarantee, with no share capital', with Barclay Inglis as chairman, Graham Searle as director, and Richard Sandbrook as Secretary. Existing UK wildlife and countryside bodies were 'charities', and received substantial tax advantages; but FoE did not even apply for charitable status. In law 'charities' could not work for political change; but that was precisely what the founders of FoE had in mind. In October 1970, Graham together with the other first fulltimers, Jonathan Holliman and Janet Whelan, moved into a miniscule office in King Street, Covent Garden, provided by Ballantine Books. A commission to compile and edit a UK edition of Ballantine's *Environmental Handbook* gave the embryo FoE Ltd its first income.

The early months were devoted to meetings with incipient Friends, and to research, to identify appropriate issues and prepare FoE campaigns. Such careful attention to detail was to become a FoE hallmark: FoE always did its homework. The powerful British mining corporation Rio Tinto-Zinc was proposing to dig a vast hole in the Snowdonia National Park, to extract copper. Graham, Brower's American representative Amory Lovins, and an Australian geologist named Simon Millar began to compile a case against the RTZ plan.

Meanwhile Cadbury-Schweppes, the largest soft-drink manufacturer in the UK, was switching over from returnable to non-returnable bottles. The Friends seized on this improbable motif as a symbol of the environmentally misguided. After attempting without success to obtain an audience with the chairman of Schweppes, the Friends took to the street. On a sunny Saturday in May 1971 a procession of a hundred Friends returned 1,500 non-returnable bottles to Schweppes headquarters. The striking visual metaphor – a forecourt entirely covered with discarded glassware – received press and TV coverage not only nationally but internationally. FoE's Schweppes 'demo' gave the word a novel slant: instead of a bitter, even ugly confrontation, it was witty and engaging – though no less serious for its lightness. The Friends stressed that their bottle-return merely illustrated a much deeper point: the accelerating waste and misuse of resources in industrial society.

The idea struck a chord. In the ensuing weeks groups calling themselves 'Friends of the Earth' suddenly sprang up all over the UK. The King Street team, caught utterly by surprise, were run off their feet simply locating and contacting this spontaneous mushrooming of local FoE groups. The FoE Ltd company papers made no provision for any such development. The King Street team had to break it to new-found Friends that 'Friends of the Earth' was a registered company name and protected by law; but King Street was willing in effect to licence use of the name by local groups sharing the same aims and ground-rules as FoE Ltd. Thus began what soon became a nationwide network of FoE local groups, a grassroots movement of remarkable stamina and resilience.

FoE's innovative campaign style attracted the enthusiasm of

advertising agencies offering to design posters and other material. The set of four Schweppes posters published by FoE in June 1971, with slogans like 'DON'T LET THEM SCHHH . . . ON BRITAIN', not only adorned many a wall but were reproduced repeatedly in the trade press, winning FoE yet more publicity. In October 1971, when Schweppes still refused to meet with FoE, the Friends repeated their bottle-return – this time simultaneously at eight different Schweppes depots around the country, the first coordinated national 'demo' involving the new local groups. The bad publicity generated by FoE at length forced the chairman of Schweppes to agree to meet with FoE Ltd to discuss the bottle business. The outcome was a national one-day conference on packaging and the environment, and a National Packaging Day in March 1972, to highlight the foolish extravagance of much modern packaging.

But back to RTZ: widespread opposition to its plans for Snowdonia had prompted it to invite Lord Zuckerman to chair an independent 'Commission on Mining and the Environment'. In January 1972 FoE submitted evidence to the Zuckerman commission, a closely-argued document entitled *Rock Bottom: Nearing the Limits of Metal Mining in Britain*, subsequently published in full in *The Ecologist* magazine. A spate of media criticism of RTZ's plans reached its peak with a BBC 'Horizon' programme called 'Do You Dig National Parks?', for which FoE had supplied considerable assistance. Its transmission in May 1972 was followed by a live studio debate in which Graham and Amory gave two senior RTZ executives a rough ride. RTZ realised it had a battle on its hands.

While mounting its challenges to Schweppes and RTZ, FoE was also embarking on a third campaign, to protect endangered wild-life. There were to be sure already a number of well-established animal-protection bodies in the UK. But Angela King, FoE's first wildlife campaigner, noted one serious gap. No other UK group was working toward control of the international trade in endangered species and products made from them. FoE began investigating imports of endangered species, focusing first on the rare big cats. FoE's reputation for scrupulous research and effective lobbying prompted approaches from experienced Parliamentary draftsmen. Soon Angela was engaged on devising the first of a succession of Endangered Species Bills. In March 1972 FoE achieved its first clearcut victory, when the Government announced a ban on the import of skins from snow leopard, clouded leopard and tiger.

In December 1971 FoE had begun contributing a monthly newsletter to *The Ecologist*. At the UN Conference on the Human

Environment, which took place in Stockholm in June 1972, FoE Ltd teamed up with *The Ecologist* and with Friends from Sweden, France and the US to produce a daily newspaper called the *Stockholm Conference Eco*. By the end of the conference the *Eco* had become required reading. It was the first of a series of *Eco*s to which FoE Ltd was to contribute; indeed the concept proved so seductive that the UN took it over and institutionalised it. In the UK, meanwhile, David Brower and other Friends, with the help of FoE Ltd, had launched a new publishing imprint, 'Earth Island', whose first title was the landmark *Limits to Growth*. However, despite an initial list of impressive quality, Earth Island fell foul of business problems and failed to establish itself commercially.

Other FoE publications met with more success; some indeed became classics of their kind. The first such was FoE's *Whale Manual*, published in June 1972 to coincide with the annual meeting of the International Whaling Commission. It was quintessential FoE material. It included a history of whaling, whale biology and population dynamics, the current state of the world whaling industry, whale products and their markets, the substitutes available, and guidelines for campaigning: that is, the relevant scientific, economic and political data, and information on how best to make use of it on behalf of the whales. The *Whale Manual* went through repeated revisions in later years, as the campaign progressed; but it remained the key document for Friends of the whale.

FoE and other whale defenders also mounted a demonstration at the IWC, the first of many; the demonstration attracted worldwide media coverage, and turned the spotlight on what would thenceforth be an acutely controversial annual gathering. A FoE Early Day Motion calling for a ban on the import of whale meat and other products was signed by 224 MPs. In July 1972 David Bowie did a benefit concert for FoE at the Royal Festival Hall, an encouraging precedent; many other celebrities were in due course to perform for FoE or take part in FoE campaigns and fund-raising. The financial boost was timely; by mid-1972 FoE had 40 local groups and eight full-time staff. The whale campaign gained further momentum from a rally in Trafalgar Square in September 1972.

The same month saw the publication of the Zuckerman report on mining and the environment. As FoE had forecast, the report ducked the issue of RTZ's proposed copper mine in Snowdonia, neither endorsing nor rejecting the proposal. Media comment was hostile, much of it directed to points raised by FoE. RTZ had meanwhile intervened at the last minute to halt publication of *Eryri*, *the Mountains of Longing,* by Amory Lovins and Philip Evans. RTZ claimed that Amory's commentary on the Snowdonia issue was actionable, and Allen & Unwin withdrew the book even as the first warm reviews appeared in the press. The book was finally published in November 1972, with an insert by RTZ; the dispute probably amplified rather than muted the book's impact. At the beginning of 1973 FoE submitted detailed evidence to the Government-appointed Stevens committee on National Parks.

By this time FoE was finding other campaign issues demanding involvement: for instance transport. In December 1972, after Prime Minister Edward Heath got caught in traffic, FoE seized the opportunity to deliver a gift-wrapped bicycle to No. 10 Downing Street, with an enormous Christmas card. The gift was declined, but pictures of it made front pages all over the world. It was the first shot in what would later become a major FoE campaign. More seriously, the following month FoE published its *Maplin Manifesto*, lending its voice to the chorus of protest at official plans to site a third London airport on the Essex coast. In March, after much internal discussion, FoE endorsed Labour candidates for election to the Greater London Council, because of Labour's opposition to plans for inner-London motorways. Labour won, and the plans were stopped; but the FoE endorsement created so much dissension within FoE, and so much antagonism from friends in other parties, that FoE thereafter stoutly refrained from further party-political forays.

March 1973 also brought the first victory in the whale campaign, when the Government announced a ban on the import of products from baleen whales. In June FoE organized a whale-poster competition for school-children in Battersea Park, in the presence of a life-size inflatable whale, and picketed the IWC conference again. *The Times* ran an ad put together by FoE, calling for a ten-year moratorium on whaling, and signed by the Duke of Edinburgh, Julian Huxley, Konrad Lorenz and other notables.

April 1973 had seen the first conference of FoE local group coordinators, with 29 groups represented. The conference was to become the biggest event on the annual FoE calendar. The same month FoE published the long-promised packaging manual, with an inimitable Searle title: *Packaging in Britain: A Policy for Containment*, by Graham Searle and Walt Patterson. It moved the Schweppes campaign on to a much broader front; for many months it was quoted and discussed not only in the popular media but also in the trade press. April also saw the culmination of one of FoE's original campaigns, in a major victory – albeit one that at first went almost unnoticed. On Easter Thursday – with no papers the next day – RTZ published its annual report; buried deep within it was the announcement that RTZ had abandoned its plans to mine copper in Snowdonia. The FoE team, like their friends in North Wales, could scarcely believe the news; but a planned council of war in Snowdonia that Easter weekend turned instead into exultant celebrations.

In May Walt Patterson and Colin Blythe from Poland Street travelled to Dundee to meet with Scottish FoE and Conservation Society members concerned about the headlong rush to develop North Sea oil, and the impact this might have on Scotland, Orkney and Shetland. They agreed to form a North Sea Oil Coalition to monitor developments and exchange information. They learned that the Government, the oil companies and the construction companies were planning to take over coastal locations for building sites for vast concrete oil-production platforms. One such site was a hamlet of 13 houses, called Drumbuie, on Loch Carron, across from the Isle of Skye. In September Walt visited the West Highlands and arranged that FoE should be the London contact for the South West Ross Action Group, to oppose the Drumbuie platform-site plan.

By that September of 1973 there were 73 local groups; one even had a full-time coordinator. FoE's lawyer, David Pedley, greeted the Government's Control of Pollution Bill by drafting 150 amendments. In October Friends staged a demo at the Motor Show; and OPEC underlined the FoE argument about the unwisdom of dependence on the car by quadrupling the price of oil. FoE was quicker to respond than any official body; at a Royal Society energy conference Friends circulated copies of *World Energy Strategies* by Amory Lovins – written before the OPEC shock. The press conference for its publication was attended by most of the Fleet Street science correspondents. It turned into a two-hour seminar led by Amory and Walt, in which the FoE pair spelled out the problems facing the light-water reactors of the US nuclear programme. Two weeks earlier the *Guardian* had revealed that the CEGB were planning to abandon British reactors in favour of Westinghouse pressurised-water reactors; and Walt had been interviewed on 'The World Tonight' on BBC Radio 4, much to the annoyance of the National Nuclear Corporation. Amory followed up the press conference with a half-page article in *The Sunday Times*; and suddenly, for the first time, there was a national public debate about nuclear power in the UK.

The Parliamentary Select Committee on Science and Technology held hearings in which the CEGB revealed that it wanted to order 32 1300-megawatt PWRs by 1983. Uproar followed. Amory and Walt prepared a 45-page memorandum on PWRs for the Select Committee; it was published in February 1974, as the first appendix to the Committee's severely critical report. The miners' strike and the three-day week led to a snap election and a change of government; and at length, after further months of controversy, in July 1974, the Labour Government rejected both the PWR and the scale of programme proposed. It gave the go-ahead for just six reactors of a British heavy-water design. Two years later this design too was to be rejected. The UK nuclear programme was collapsing in disarray, with FoE in the thick of the fray.

While stirring up trouble for the nuclear industry, FoE and the local groups were also challenging official oil policy, and the plans of the Conservative Government to 'nationalize' the site at Drumbuie. With the change of government in February 1974 this legislation fell. In April Walt testified for FoE at the Drumbuie inquiry, pointing out that official plans would lead to platform-sites becoming derelict within a few years – a conclusion subsequently fully borne out. In August 1974, thanks to the efforts of the National Trust for Scotland, the South West Ross Action Group, FoE and other objectors, the Government turned down the Drumbuie application – though it almost immediately accepted another on the north side of the Loch.

In November 1973 Graham departed for New Zealand, amid a flurry of concern lest his going would leave FoE leaderless. The concern proved unwarranted. Richard Sandbrook became director, adopting a much lower profile, and leaving campaigns in the hands of the individual campaigners themselves, who were by this time amply experienced in all the various roles they had to play. Angela King arranged to deliver to the Japanese and the Russians a petition calling for them to cease their whaling activities, signed by leading figures in European management and labour. FoE's Endangered Species Bill received its First Reading in December 1973 and its Second Reading in January 1974, defeating the Government in the process. The election intervened; but the Bill was at once reintroduced, and in March 1974 received a First Reading for the second time. It still, however, had a long and convoluted Parliamentary road ahead of it.

March 1974 also saw the publication of Pete Wilkinson's *Campaigners' Manual*, an activist's guide to action. On Housewarming Weekend some 50 local groups insulated the homes of pensioners, to launch what was to become one of FoE's longest-running and most telling campaigns. The thermal insulation campaign, initiated and carried out almost entirely by the local groups, demonstrated that FoE was not interested only in 'stopping things': that as well as opposing environment malfeasance it was taking positive action to bring about improvements. Another long-running affirmative campaign was also launched that same month. Poland Street and the local groups built 40 towering 'paper mountains', including one in the forecourt of the Greater London Council, to kick off The Great Paper Chase, to collect and recycle the hundreds of thousands of tons of paper wasted every year. The FoE Paper Chase was all too successful. By 1975 so much waste paper was being collected that the paper mills could not cope with it. The economic recession depressed the market for paper, the price of waste paper plummeted, and many local FoE groups which had come to rely on the income from paper collection found themselves in financial trouble. FoE accordingly redirected its campaigning efforts toward persuading paper buyers to specify recycled paper, in order to build up a market; but it was uphill work.

For the IWC conference in June 1974 Angela and her allies arranged to have a life-size inflatable whale float down the Thames. Japanese and Russian delegates were to be invited to aim a harpoon gun at it from the Embankment. Unfortunately, the floating whale sprang a leak and began to sink. Thames River Police had to come to the rescue with adhesive tape. Angela and the others returned crestfallen to Poland Street; but the sinking whale proved to be a picture editor's dream, and made front pages all over the world – with captions underlining the obvious metaphorical import. The apparent fiasco turned into one of FoE's most effective pieces of theatre.

In July 1974 FoE published *Losing Ground*, by Colin Blythe, a critique of land-use and agricultural policy in the UK. It was followed in November by *Britain and the World Food Crisis*, a brief FoE paper which provoked unexpected outrage by noting the amount of food consumed by British pets – one of the infrequent instances of maladroit FoE public relations. At the UN Food Conference in Rome FoE helped to publish a newspaper called *Pan*, which contrasted the comfortable aura of the conference with the plight of the ill-fed. That same month FoE made a conscious decision to step outside its well-established groundrule, and break the law: by taking over a derelict bomb-site near the Old Vic and turning it into an allotment. The allotments campaign was taken up with vigour by FoE local groups, calling upon local authorities to fulfil their legal obligations to make land available. In March 1975 FoE published the *Allotments Manual*.

In January 1975 FoE's Endangered Species Bill was introduced for the third time; and the Wild Creatures and Wild Plants Bill, drafted by FoE's lawyer David Pedley, dealing with the protection of domestic species, was given a First Reading. The second edition of the *Whale Manual* was published, as was a revised edition of *Losing Ground*.

Mick Hamer's study of the roads lobby, *Wheels Within Wheels*, had been published by FoE in October 1974; in February 1975 he joined the Poland Street staff as full-time transport campaigner. In June FoE published *Give Way*, the cycle campaign manual, and linked up with other organizations for Bike Day. The police decreed that cycling along Whitehall would be 'too dangerous'; so 3000 cyclists wheeled their bikes past Downing Street, along the Embankment and over Westminster Bridge to a mass rally. The rally and the many events staged by local FoE groups received massive media coverage; thenceforth the bicycle was always identified as the Friendliest vehicle. Motorways, however, were clearly unFriendly. At the M16 inquiry Mick and John Adams launched a FoE attack on official road traffic forecasts, which was soon to have a profound influence on road planning.

On the energy front, the Royal Commission on Environmental Pollution had embarked on a two-year investigation of nuclear power. In December 1974 FoE published its RCEP evidence as *Nuclear Power: Technical Bases for Ethical Concern*, by Amory Lovins. Yet more controversy greeted *Dynamic Energy Analysis and Nuclear Power*, by John Price, which suggested that the rapid buildup of nuclear capacity then anticipated would actually consume more energy than it supplied. The validity of the argument was never tested, because the buildup never materialised. December also brought Bottle Day, involving 70 FoE groups, and the publication of the FoE recycling manual, *Material Gains*, by Christine Thomas.

By this time Tom Burke had moved from Merseyside FoE to Poland Street, to become the first full-time national coordinator of local groups. In January 1975 62 local groups attended the third Coordinators' Conference; and in March FoE groups from twelve countries sent representatives to the FoE International meeting in London. The pattern of decentralised cooperative campaigning in the UK had begun to extend across national boundaries, with Friends in different countries working together on issues of common concern, like energy and whales. In April 1975 Friends from several European countries, the UK included, met with EEC energy bureaucrats in Brussels to put the FoE viewpoint. In June, Friends from other countries joined FoE UK outside the IWC conference, to take part in a funeral ceremony for the whales. It may have been conceived as street theatre, but those who took part emerged shaken and moved.

By 1975 the Poland Street office was itself becoming an environmental wasteland, overcrowded, noisy, and suffocating under its own detritus. After lengthy discussions the Board decided to activate plans to put FoE's research work under the wing of a separate, charitable body – and under a separate roof. Graham Searle, back from New Zealand, took on the task of establishing Earth Resources Research. Poland Street staff working on research rather than campaigns moved with Graham to new premises at 40, James Street, and those left behind in Poland Street took their first deep breaths for months. By this time FoE and ERR together had 18 full-time staff.

In May 1975 FoE held a tenth birthday party in Belgravia for the still-unfinished Dungeness B nuclear station. At the party FoE published a tabloid *Nuclear Times*. One of its front-page articles described plans to expand reprocessing at Windscale, and to service foreign customers, which would make Windscale 'one of the world's main radioactive dustbins'. Five months later the *Daily Mirror* picked up the story and ran a black front page headline: 'PLAN TO MAKE BRITAIN WORLD'S NUCLEAR DUSTBIN'. Furore ensued, with FoE again prominent. In another innovation Poland Street and the local groups in November 1975 arranged the first of what were to become regular 'Campaign Workshops'. The workshops were to bring together full-time campaigners with local-group members wanting to focus their efforts on a particular campaign, raising the level of expertise in the local groups and helping Poland Street to keep in step with the realities of local-group campaigning. Energy was a fortunate choice for the first Workshop; the Windscale campaign was to last three years and cost FoE close to £100,000, stretching Poland Street and the local groups to the limit of their resources.

After British Nuclear Fuels Ltd staged a public debate in London, FoE decided to return the compliment, chartered a train and filled it to capacity for a 'Nuclear Excursion' to Windscale in April 1976; MPs, BNFL staff and union representatives and Friends met on the football pitch outside the security fence for a day-long debate. Throughout the summer and autumn FoE continued to press for the Windscale application to be called in for a public inquiry. Publication of the Royal Commission report – the 'Flowers report' – in September powerfully reinforced public concern about reprocessing, plutonium and the fast breeder reactor, long since the focus of the FoE campaign. *Nuclear Prospects* by Mike Flood and Robin

Grove-White, co-published by FoE, the CPRE and the NCCL in October 1976, stirred yet more concern about the social and political implications of the planned 'plutonium economy'. By December 1976 the national outcry was unanswerable; on 22 December the Secretary of State for the Environment announced that there would be a public inquiry into the Windscale plan.

While the energy campaign erupted into the headlines, FoE's wildlife campaign was recording a memorable victory. In November 1976, after four years, the *Endangered Species Act* reached the Statute books, severely restricting trade in many endangered species and products made from them. Other campaigns too continued to evolve. In August 1976 FoE published *Getting Nowhere Fast* by Mick Hamer, a remarkable study of mobility in modern society, as a response to the Government's consultation document on transport. The Government's White Paper on Transport, published in May 1977, reflected marked FoE influence, for instance including a commitment to reducing the amount of movement required in the UK. In June 1977 British Rail announced free rail carriage for bicycles, another victory for FoE and its cycling colleagues.

In the run-up to the Windscale Inquiry FoE UK joined with Friends from several other countries, and with many others opposed to nuclear developments, to stage the first international conference of nuclear opponents, in Salzburg, Austria, in April 1977. Called 'Conference for a Non-Nuclear Future', it took place just a block away from the vast International Atomic Energy Agency conference on 'Nuclear Energy and its Fuel Cycle'. The Non-Nuclear conference shook the IAEA delegates when a Non-Nuclear speaker revealed for the first time that 200 tonnes of uranium had been stolen in 1968, and that the responsible authorities had covered up the theft for nine years. The story made headlines all over the world.

In early June FoE and Earth Resources Research published *The Fissile Society* by Walt Patterson, a study of the social and economic implications of electronuclear plans. A week later, on 14 June, the Windscale Inquiry got under way at Whitehaven, Cumbria. By the time it ended, after exactly 100 days of sittings, in November 1977, FoE's participation had been widely acclaimed. Even before the Inquiry ended, FoE and the Atomic Energy Authority had been co-sponsors of a two-day public conference at the Royal Institution in which, for virtually the first time, a large group of environmentalists and a large group of nuclear proponents came together, each discovering that the other did not have two heads. It was probably the high-water mark of the dialogue in the UK nuclear debate; five months later the Parker report on Windscale shattered any illusions about the force of rational argument on nuclear issues. Ironically, the efforts of Poland Street and the local groups from November 1977 to March 1978 were concentrated on achieving publication of the report, and Parliamentary debate on it, before any Government decision. FoE helped to marshall irresistible pressure to this end. Alas for the efforts: the report proved to be a numbing dismissal of every opposition argument, and could have been written without even holding the inquiry.

In the aftermath FoE published a bitter critique called *The Parker Inquiry*, detailing the inadequacy of the official report. The Parker report polarized the nuclear issue in the UK essentially beyond any hope of recovery. The Windscale Rally at the end of April, organized by Poland Street with heroic support from the FoE local groups and many others, brought over 12,000 people in a mass procession from Marble Arch to Trafalgar Square. It was the largest gathering of nuclear opponents in the UK since the heyday of the old Campaign for Nuclear Disarmament; and it presaged an upsurge of popular anger about nuclear issues of every kind – civil and military alike.

The Windscale issue absorbed the energies of FoE to an extent previously unparalleled, for well over a year; but other FoE campaigns continued unperturbed. In January 1978 FoE's otter campaign scored a victory, winning protection for otters in England and Wales. The official Leitch report on traffic planning, published that month, was a scathing attack on the Government's traffic forecasting methods, fully vindicating FoE's long-running onslaught on the Department of Transport. In April 1978 FoE published the *Bicycle Planning Book*, which at once became a specialised bestseller among local planning authorities, not only in the UK but internationally. In June 1978 Mike Oldfield played a benefit concert for FoE and the whales, to an audience of 3,000.

In September FoE prosecuted an importer of the hawksbill turtle under the Endangered Species Act. The case was lost on a technicality but prompted changes in the law to close loopholes. In January 1979 FoE won its first such case, against an importer trying to sell a leopard skin illegally imported into the UK. In November 1978 FoE laid the foundations for similar legal challenges in another area, with the publication of *Polluters Pay* by FoE's lawyer Richard Macrory, an action guide to the Control of Pollution Act. In February 1979 FoE won its case against an application for a 'hypermarket' in Nottingham, which would have depended entirely on cars for its custom.

On the energy front FoE had gained national recognition for its commitment to energy conservation. FoE Durham had pioneered the idea of using funds from the Manpower Services Commission to hire unemployed youngsters and put them to work insulating the homes of pensioners and others in damp, draughty dwellings. Soon many local FoE groups were running insulation programmes, so successfully that the Department of the Environment endorsed the approach in a circular to local authorities, and Ministers speaking in the House of Commons acknowledged the value of FoE's contribution. In January 1978 100 FoE groups staged conservation events. Poland Street published *Rethink Electric* by Czech Conroy, and followed it with *Torness: Keep It Green* by Mike Flood, both stressing the existing surplus of power station capacity and challenging the necessity for new plant. The economic arguments against nuclear investment were thus just beginning to come to the fore, when the accident at Three Mile Island in Pennsylvania catapulted safety back into the headlines.

Earlier that year, in March, FoE declared itself in favour of one kind of *Economic Growth*, by publishing, under this title, its allotments campaign manual. British Rail attempted to ban bikes on Southern Region, but dropped the ban in the face of protests by FoE and other cycling groups. The informal cyclists' coalition went on the offensive in June, as 6,000 people got on their bikes to 'Reclaim the Road', leaving a Trafalgar Square rally in a torrent that filled Whitehall from side-to-side and end-to-end for half an hour, to the fury of its four-wheeled presumptive owners. A month later FoE was back in Trafalgar Square, as 12,000 people gathered to Save the Whale. By this time FoE's campaign for a ban on the import of sperm oil had massive all-party support in Parliament, and even the IWC was at last giving ground. The UK Government agreed to press for an EEC ban on all whale products; and the IWC declared the Indian Ocean a whale sanctuary.

In the early weeks of the new Conservative Government, FoE people met with several Ministers, including those in the Department of Energy, and prepared an invited briefing on the role of private generation of electricity. But the Government's nuclear fixation soon became evident, culminating in its statement of December 1979 calling for 10 PWRs to be ordered by 1992. FoE responded by launching in March 1980 a five-year campaign of opposition, kicked off by a 'Harrisburg Day' rally bringing 15,000 people to Trafalgar Square, and by publication of Mike Flood's popular polemic *The Big Risk*. The new Parliamentary Select Committee on Energy undertook hearings on the Government's nuclear policy statement; FoE prepared written and oral evidence. The Select Committee's report, in February 1981, endorsed and reiterated many of the points put forward by FoE. The following month FoE in turn published *The Pressurized Water Reactor: A Critique of the Government's Nuclear Power Programme.*

In June 1980 Friends went on safari down Knightsbridge, led by a hunter in a solar topee, in search of striped and spotted cats and other threatened species in the windows of the fashionable stores. Vigorous FoE lobbying helped to bring about EEC agreement to ban most whale products. In September FoE challenged the Government's failure to protect the otter in Scotland; in December the Government accepted FoE's case. In February 1981 FoE published *Paradise Lost: the Destruction of Britain's Wildlife Habitats*, by Czech Conroy with an introduction by David Bellamy.

Other campaigns likewise rolled on; and in May 1981 FoE UK celebrated its tenth anniversary. By this time FoE had 17,000 supporters, 250 local groups, and an annual budget of £300,000. Among the 24 national FoE organizations affiliated to Friends of the Earth International, FoE UK was one of the oldest, largest and most successful. But all was far from well. The effects of tight finances and over-extended resources had contributed to some internal friction. Some people even wondered whether, a decade old, FoE had outlived its usefulness – whether the Friends should agree to go their separate ways.

Matters came to a head at a special conference in October 1981, with FoE Birmingham, one of the strongest local groups, as hosts. Poland Street staff, Board members, and representatives from local groups all over the country convened a meeting that all knew would be crucial. Memories of the acrimony that had tainted recent coordinators' conferences made many participants acutely apprehensive. Would this be the weekend when Friends became foes?

The discussions were intense; few punches were pulled. But the results astonished even the most cynical participants. In two days of deliberations Friends of the Earth created a complete new structure for the organization. The local groups would be invited to elect members to the Board. The Board, in formulating FoE policy and in staffing the new FoE Ltd office, would thus be responsible to the local groups. The concept had to be taken back to the groups, discussed, modified and endorsed. Difficult decisions remained. But it meant a new era for the Friends. They had arrived in Birmingham wondering whether a decade of effort was coming to an end. They left feeling that a decade of effort was just beginning – and that, whatever the problems to come, Friends of the Earth would meet them head on. It was the reaffirmation of a beautiful Friendship.

DES WILSON
10 FoE: Today and tomorrow

TO FULLY APPRECIATE the legacy left by the
founders of FoE in Britain, many of whom are still involved in
environmental campaigning, it is necessary to look at the variety of
activities that have preoccupied the movement more recently, for
instance, in the year 1983. . . .

Once more we were involved in a campaign on nuclear energy,
this time endeavouring to block the plans of the Central Electricity
Generating Board, warmly supported by Energy Ministers, to
introduce a pressurized water reactor to Britain – to be precise, at
Sizewell in East Anglia. FoE concentrated on safety. Its case was
that the PWR should not be built because the CEGB's safety standards
and criteria were inadequate; that the design as proposed did not
even meet those inadequate standards; that the CEGB prediction that
the reactor (the same as that at Three Mile Island) would be nearly
1,000 times safer than American PWRs had been shown to be wishful
thinking and could not be achieved in practice; that the CEGB had
not resolved 80 outstanding safety issues, a number of which were
crucial; and that it would contribute to a situation in which intensified
international competition for nuclear reactor export orders could
lead to a relaxation of safeguards on nuclear technology with a

resulting increase in the number of countries using reactors as a route to nuclear weapons.

The public inquiry took place at Snape Maltings under the Chairmanship of Sir Frank Layfield. From the start FoE alleged that the inquiry was financially fixed, because the Secretary of State for Energy, Nigel Lawson (later to become Chancellor of the Exchequer) refused public funding for objectors, although the CEGB was said to be spending up to £10 million of electricty consumers' money on the inquiry. Anyone who made the journey to Snape Maltings and who saw the huge contingent of expensive lawyers and technical experts on the CEGB side, and often only one or two lonely researchers at the objectors' tables, could see how unsatisfactory it was. It became apparent early on that FoE simply could not afford to be fully involved in the Inquiry and we then had to decide whether it was better to boycott it altogether. This would have been an honourable position and would have been consistent with our view that the Inquiry was intended to reach only one result. If a boycott by objectors was unanimous, it would also have made the Inquiry even more obviously a farce and thus embarrass both Lawson and the CEGB. However, a number of objectors decided, albeit with reservations, that their criticisms of the PWR were sufficiently valid for them to be able to made a dent in the CEGB case, even with limited resources, and that they must take the opportunity of the Inquiry to do so. Thus there was no possibility of a unified boycott. FoE, too, felt it could make a considerable impact with the evidence it could produce that the PWR was unsafe, and that it could do this by limited participation in the Inquiry. The decision whether or not to proceed was a finely balanced one, but we proceeded for four reasons.

1.   The PWR was demonstrably unsafe, and the Inquiry did create a platform on which we could publicise the evidence for this.

2.   Given the thick skin of Mr Lawson (and his successor, Peter Walker), it was unlikely that the absence of objectors at the Inquiry would stop the Minister from accepting its recommendations. On the contrary, both Lawson and Walker were perfectly capable of claiming that this proved the lack of public concern and the lack of a real case on the other side. It was necessary that the evidence be placed on the record.

3.   Participation in the Inquiry put FoE in a position to demand information and force facts out of the CEGB that otherwise would have remained secret.

4.   While opinion was divided, many supporters wanted us to

participate, and were prepared to raise the money to do so. If we did not respond to that demand, we would not have proved to be the vehicle our supporters needed to act on their concerns.

FoE's groups and supporters were magnificent and raised around £100,000 so that FoE could participate. FoE's first achievement was to expose the fact that the Nuclear Installations Inspectorate had failed to complete and publicise its view of crucial safety questions in time for the Inquiry, despite promises by Ministers that this would be done. FoE cross-examined the CEGB on safety issues in the autumn of 1983 and as 1984 dawned (and this book went to press) was preparing to call its own witnesses.

To raise the money and to participate in such a major inquiry would alone be a reasonable achievement in one year but this was only part of FoE's programme in 1983. On the energy front, we published two books: one, *Solar Prospects* by former FoE campaigner, Mike Flood, offered an alternative to conventional sources of energy; the other, *The PWR Decision: How Not To Buy A Nuclear Reactor* by Renee Chudleigh and William Cannell, provided an account of the world nuclear export scene.

FoE also collaborated with Greenpeace and transport unions in meetings and activities on the issue of dumping of nuclear waste at sea and exposed secret Ministry of Defence dumping plans. There was a campaign to publicise the benefits of combined heat and power (CHP) and a major countryside campaign with over 60 local groups engaged in monitoring the country's 3,877 Sites of Special Scientific Interest and defending smaller, more typical features of the countryside under threat. We produced our own proposals for a new law to replace the disastrous 1981 Wildlife and Countryside Act.

Typical of the FoE approach to campaigning were the activities of Joe Weston and other Oxfordshire Friends. In their fight to stop the M40 motorway destroying one of Britain's most famous fields at Otmoor, they had the field divided into thousands of plots and sold these to environmentalists around the world in order to make it extremely difficult for compulsory purchase orders to be served. Other countryside campaigners were involved in a battle to save Seal Sands, the last 400 acres of inter-tidal and mud-flats on the Tees estuary in County Cleveland. Rye Friends were campaigning to save oak trees on land farmed by the leader of the local district council. Thurrock Friends were campaigning to save Colehouse Fort marshes under threat from tipping in Essex. And on the Surrey and Hampshire border, Friends were involved in protecting a Site of

Special Scientific Interest called St Catherine's Down, under threat from the M3 extension. There were scores of similar campaigns.

A tropical rain forest campaign was being launched towards the end of the year and FoE also took an active part in lobbying the International Whaling Commission's meeting in Brighton. In the summer FoE launched a major report and campaign on straw-burning by farmers and achieved widespread publicity and a governmental inquiry. While FoE members were involved in the annual Great British Bicycle Ride (from Lands End to John O'Groats), and FoE was continuing to lobby Ministers and local authorities on behalf of the cyclist, transport campaigner, Don Mathew, was preparing a major drive to build up support to protect public transport from further cut-backs. FoE Director, Steve Billcliffe, joined local campaigners to force CEGB to take proper precautionary measures to stop the dispersal of asbestos when old power stations were demolished. A research project was under way on acid rain and a campaign in preparation. Scores of FoE groups joined up with CLEAR, The Campaign for Lead-free Air, and won a major victory when Ministers were forced to concede the principle of lead-free petrol. A big research project was organised to back up a pesticides campaign to be launched in 1984.

When the election took place in June, all candidates received a FoE questionnaire and over 800 replied, 580 of them being declared by FoE 'environmentally-acceptable candidates'. The Prime Minister replied but failed to pass the test! The legendary American consumer and environmental campaigner, Ralph Nader, came across the Atlantic to spearhead three days of FoE rallies and events around Britain. These were a tremendous success, with the Central Hall, Westminster (capacity 2,500 people), being filled twice in one day. A FoE newspaper was launched with plans to develop it as a quarterly and then develop it further.

At the same time, FoE groups all over the country were involved in their own activities, either campaigning locally on national issues, or involving themselves in local environmental controversies. The pioneering work of Walt Patterson, Graham Searle, Richard Sandbrook, and the others over that first 10 years had, then, not been in vain. FoE had become a versatile, knowledgeable and popular campaign and – to pick up where Walt's chapter left off – had also become united behind a strategy developed within the movement and calculated to carry the campaign forward for the remainder of the decade. That strategy has a number of strands. . . .

First, FoE believes that you cannot change the world if your own lifestyle does not reflect the ideals you advocate. Therefore, we have sought a structure within FoE and a way of working together that reflects the kind of society we would like to live in. All FoE groups are autonomous, taking their own decision on their particular role in their community, on whether or not to participate in national campaigns, and on their own campaigning style. Some like to become involved in practical work, others in campaigning, others in fund-raising, others in life-style experiments, and some in a mix of two or more of these. The central headquarters is also autonomous, and can carry out its own pressure group activities. However, if it hopes to have the support of the movement, it has to win that support by persuasion. The majority of its Board members are elected democra-tically on a regional basis and this increases the influence of the movement on decisions on overall policy. A bigger full-time FoE group like that in Birmingham operates on a cooperative basis and FoE generally seeks to avoid hierarchical structures. Despite some bad spells in the past, we seek to solve our problems by friendly and generous discussion.

Second, FoE honestly acknowledges the limitations of any organisation in the face of the environmental crisis. There is no way that we alone can reverse the tide of environmental destruction and the squandering of resources. Therefore, we seek to fit within a greater picture. Those who devote their energies entirely to party politics often argue that pressure groups like FoE look at issues on too narrow a base, and that only by obtaining political power to achieve radical economic and social change can we achieve our ideals. Of course FoE accepts the need for political change, but if we assume that radical political change cannot happen in less than a decade, then the continuation of present political policies will have by then created irreversible damage. For instance, the nuclear power programme will have proceeded beyond the point where it can easily be stopped. Public transport could be run down to the point where the car has achieved total dominance. Thousands and thousands of acres of countryside could be desecrated and wildlife habitats lost forever. The key to effective involvement is to find ways of influencing policies and priorities now, whilst awaiting more fundamental political change later.

Over the past couple of years we have sought to stress the 'triple approach': maintaining the role of FoE as a specialist pressure group for environmental protection and conservation; establishing links and sympathetically supporting other parts of the green movement, most notably the peace movement and the world developmental movement; and as individuals participating in political parties of our choice to seek to relate what we have learned and what we know from our pressure group activity to the wider political scene.

The research we do within FoE, and practical experience on the ground, means that we have more to contribute to the political parties we join than untested theory. By establishing links with the green movement as a whole, we can look for more effective intermediate action. For instance, FoE is not a direct supporter of CND, because its members vary in their support for multilateral or unilateral disarmament, but we are supportive of the peace movement, and we make our contribution by stressing the relationship between nuclear energy and the proliferation of nuclear weapons, and on this issue we have worked with CND.

Acknowledging its limitations of resources, FoE increasingly attempts to set up or join coalitions with other organisations. In order to confront the worldwide problem of over-use and mis-use of pesticides, FoE has joined a number of British environmental and overseas aid organisations under the banner of the Pesticides Action Network. Each contributes resources to a major research project that will lead to a campaign being launched in 1984 and continued throughout the Eighties to achieve statutory controls on pesticide use and to maintain surveillance on the issue. Working as a coalition, we expect to achieve more input and be able to exert more political pull than would otherwise be the case.

FoE is also involved in cooperative action with other countryside and wildlife groups within an informal organisation called 'Wildlife Link'. It joins with other transport groups on the Board of Transport 2000. On the Sizewell PWR Inquiry, FoE, the Council for Protection of Rural England, the Stop Sizewell B Association, and others, came together to plan joint press conferences and to divide between them the different aspects of the Inquiry they would concentrate on, in order that each could use its resources to maximum effect.

Frustrated by the difficulty in obtaining information from a governmental system constructed around an obsession with secrecy, FoE has initiated a major coalition to achieve greater freedom of information. Launched in early 1984 under the title 'The 1984 Campaign for Freedom of Information', it too has attracted funds from a variety of pressure groups, and thus been able to make a far greater impact than FoE could ever have hoped to do alone.

This leads me to another strand in the FoE strategy – to seek to run or support campaigns that relate to structural weaknesses in society. We support efforts to make bureaucracies more accountable, to make the country more democratic, to give people more influence over their own lives. What has this to do with environmental issues? The answer is that much of the damage is being done by non-accountable huge multi-national companies, or by governmental bureaucracies with enormous influence although little contact with the communities and environments they can affect.

FoE has also tried to evolve its own unique campaign style. As the strategy document being debated within the movement in the early 1980s stated:

> FoE seeks a correct balance between fact and feelings. It harnesses idealism to argument based on unanswerable research and positive alternatives. At the same time, we appeal with moral, aesthetic, and emotive arguments derived from our ideals. We campaign by action, for we are an initiator, in the sense that we undertake to put our principles into action. Our campaigns are human in style. We seek to mix serious debate with humour, and detailed research with imaginative action. We seek to generate positive responses from the public. We work within the spirit of the law and, at all times, reject violence.

Involvement in a movement like FoE can often be disillusioning and frustrating. All the power and wealth lies with those who seek to exploit the planet and all living things for their own short-term ends. There is no choice, however, but to do what we can. The Ecology Party in Britain is fond of quoting the words of E. F. Schumacher:

> We must do what we conceive to be the right thing, and not bother our heads or burden our souls with whether we are going to be successful. Because if we don't do the right thing, we'll be doing the wrong thing, and we will just be part of the disease, and not a part of the cure.

This is a philosophy worthy of adoption.

Fortunately, we achieve our successes and from them draw hope. As Dr. Johnson wrote, 'Where there is no hope, there can be no endeavour'. Hope is to be found in others who also see matters as we do, who also care, and who in their actions as well as their words demonstrate their desire to make the world a better place and to protect it for the generations to come. In the area of environmental concern, a movement such as Friends of the Earth offers refuge and opportunity for such people. FoE is a place where we can find hope in and with others. No one can argue that FoE is not needed. It is needed to research the problems, expose the causes, and demonstrate that there are better solutions. It is needed to educate and involve our families, neighbours, and friends and to rally them behind the cause. It is needed as part of an articulate, informed and influential opposition to the destroyers, polluters, and exploiters. It is needed as a partner to other organisations who cannot do it all alone. It is needed as a vehicle for our own idealism and shared beliefs and as a way whereby we can work together. But, above all, it is needed as a source of hope. And hope, it is said, 'ever urges on, and tells us tomorrow will be better'.

●APPENDIX

In addition to its involvement in British environmental issues, FoE in the UK supports international conservation campaigns. This special additional chapter puts FoE's wildlife campaigning in its international perspective.

CHARLES SECRETT

Wildlife:
An international perspective

ALL OUR PLANET'S continents are different, but one is completely unique. Antarctica teems with wildlife, is demilitarised by international agreement, is nuclear-free, is unpolluted and is dedicated to scientific research. It is a sanctuary for critically endangered mammal species and for hundreds of millions of other animals and birds. Embedded in its pristine geology, so far unspoilt by human activity, are probable clues to many evolutionary secrets. Its gigantic mass, spreading over 5·4 million square miles, has a dominant influence on global climates. Because of its pivotal role within the biosphere it both deserves and needs to be carefully looked after. Yet, this last-chance Eden is now at the centre of an escalating international row which threatens to do irreparable damage to its wilderness; Antarctica's wealth of wildlife is threatened and its untapped natural resources are the source of conflict.

Now from the coldest place on earth to the wettest: tropical moist forests harbour more wild species, in sheer numbers and diversity, than any other ecosystem. Estimated to contain at least 50% of all organisms, these forests are the most complex expression of life on earth. For instance, the Sunda Shelf region of South East

Asia supports at least 297 different mammal and 732 bird species, twice as many as are found in Europe (134 and 398 respectively) which is an area four times as large. One small forested volcano, Mount Makiliang in the Phillipines, contains more woody plant species than all of the US; while Panama has as many plants as Europe (see Myers, *The Sinking Ark*, further reading). All of these species are dependent on tropical moist forest systems. If the forests go, the species will disappear. And so will human beings. In the last four hundred years, Brazil's Indian population has declined from 6–9 million to just 200,000. Our planet is currently losing primary moist forests at a rate of between 5.6 and 20 million hectares per year, almost solely as a result of careless development. This amounts to an area the size of Switzerland every few months. Every day at least one species of life on earth becomes extinct. By 1990 that will probably become one an hour.

Humanity's ignorance about wildlife is remarkable. No one even knows how many species there are. So far some 1.6 million have been discovered and named. Recent estimates suggest that there may be some 30 million in all, mostly insects and arachnids (spiders). An average of 20 new insect and 15 new plant species are discovered every day. Meanwhile the pressures grow even faster.

Protecting wildlife is a complicated and intricate business. It is beset with difficulties and partial solutions. The problems of endangered species, of threatened ecosystems, even of the philosophy and purpose of conservation itself, are not easy to summarise. While there are no clear cut answers, there are common threads linking many of the more obvious dilemmas.

One thing is certain – the days of luxury wildlife conservation are over. Confronted by political developments like those governing Antarctica or tropical moist forests, environmentalists can no longer afford to concentrate on saving individual species, no matter how colourful or appealing. Blue whales, elephants or tigers must become symbols for a larger campaign, the survival of critical biomes trapped between the growing wealth of the North and the growing poverty of the South. The glittering chimera of perpetual economic growth which bedazzles developed nations, and the grim spectre of spiralling populations which haunts the undeveloped, exert all too real pressures on wildlife and their habitats. Where once the snow leopard or the peregrine falcon automatically commanded the bulk of conservation's resources now entire ecosystems must be saved. Crisis forces urgent questions on environmentalists, who are compelled to be effective at all costs. Which is the most efficient strategy – sustainable yield or outright protection? Which the most telling argument – rational pragmatism or passionate idealism? Attempts to answer these questions have led to many different conclusions.

In 1980 the US Fish and Wildlife Service embarked on a $25 million rescue programme to save one bird, the Californian condor, from extinction. Ancient, majestic and superbly evolved to soar in huge sweeps miles above the tangled chapperal and mountain ridges of its last remaining foothold, in the Serpe–Frazier Wilderness north of Santa Barbara, the Californian condor is a living fossil left over from the Pleistocene Age. Like many predators at the top of the food chain (e.g. the osprey, otter, Texas gray wolf and Mexican grizzly bear) the condor has become the victim of persistent pesticides, of poisons intended for rodents, of hunters and of the thoughtless development of its breeding and feeding grounds. Although there are deep divisions among US conservationists over the methods used by the rescue teams (captive breeding as opposed to adequate habitat protection) most believe the effort and expense justified. For them, the condor personifies many of the qualities – independence, endurance, strength, regality, even beauty, although it is an ugly thing to look at – which jolt human beings from self-centred complacency. And many feel that to let the condor disappear would be an unpardonable breach of the planet's natural protective mantle. As a living spaceship the Earth is dependent for its healthy survival on the intricate inter-relationship of all its life forms. Environmentalists Anne and Paul Erlich argue that every extinction is like popping a rivet from an aircraft: at some point the critical threshold is crossed and the wings fall off.

But others reject this analysis and believe in different methods. For them, in a world where species are disappearing so rapidly, every precious pound must be used to the widest benefit. Not all species can be saved so the most important must be. Importance should not be determined solely by concepts of 'endangeredness', but also by pragmatism – what will be lost and what gained by spending time, money, research, and people on protecting one species as opposed to another? When we stand to lose at least one million forms of life in under 20 years $25 million for one bird seems, for some, a great deal too much money. In trying to solve the larger problems of global extinctions Norman Myers, for instance, has advocated a 'triage approach' for conservation, a practice evolved by French battlefield doctors overwhelmed by casualties in the First World War. Each soldier was categorised: those who would recover with help; those who would survive without attention; and those who would die no matter how much medical care they received. The first category absorbed all available resources. The other two were ignored. Myers argues that wild species can be similarly classified. Those which are unusually vulnerable to summary extinction but which guarantee an ecosystem's stability or are of significant economic value may better justify the expenditure of scarce resources. In this way optimum numbers of species could be spared.

At first sight this appears reasonable and practical. Up to a point it is – but who chooses, and how, which species meet these criteria? Many argue that such decisions are impossible. Inevitably some species are deliberately lost – where does one draw the line? Once the private realisation that some will inevitably become extinct evolves into a public philosophy the battle is already half lost. Conservationists cannot afford to admit any species should be allowed to disappear, but must always act as if all can be saved. If it is legitimate to eradicate one, even as the indirect consequence of a useful development, then every species is vulnerable.

Traditionally, conservation organisations have relied on persuasion to prevent unnecessary exploitation. During the 1970s many groups became frustrated at the general lack of progress and took to direct action to press home their case, often with great success. The 'Save the Whale' campaign is one famous example. This tactical change is mirrored by the different attitudes that organisations have adopted in determining their role. And inevitably this has resulted in divisions between conservation and animal welfare organisations – which at best border on competitiveness or uncoordinated efforts, with groups plying their own separate courses, and at worst involves public derision of each other's methods and ideas.

Objective reasoning underpins the philosophy of the International Union for the Conservation of Nature and Natural Resources, the most important scientific non-governmental organisation. Consisting of 450 statutory and voluntary conservation groups, it was founded in 1948 to preserve 'areas, objects, fauna, flora having scientific, historic and aesthetic significance'. Respected and admired by scientists and politicians, it rigorously documents and researches invaluable information on the status of endangered species the world over, and plans its conservation strategies accordingly. By contrast, the animal welfare and rights movement, deeply affected by the barbaric exploitation of more common species like the Canadian harp seal, taps a far more immediate public response. Its overtly emotional campaigns assert the natural right of wild creatures to live unmolested and, to some extent, have curtailed ruthless and unnecessary killing.

Yet, despite widespread international revulsion, the clubbing of baby harp seals and the use of intensive livestock systems continue, political contingencies outweighing the unfocused concern of millions of people. On the other hand, the World Conservation Strategy, IUCN's blueprint for survival, which argues that conservation is an inevitable and integral component of development and not a luxury activity in its own right, has been adopted, albeit with varying degrees of commitment, by over 35 countries. Each approach has met with partial success; to decide whether one is better than the other is pointless. The lesson to be learnt is: if something works, use it.

For wildlife conservation to be effective, political and popular priorities must be bridged. As emotional and spiritual, as well as rational, animals we cannot continue to allow major conservation priorities to be determined almost entirely according to intellectual criteria. Given the enormity of the task at hand all those groups who are trying to protect threatened species must band together, no matter how loosely at first, in order to succeed.

* * *

If reaching accord on the correct approach is difficult, identifying the reasons for saving wildlife should not be. There are many sound arguments for, and practical benefits from, treating wild species and their habitats with respect – aesthetic, ecological, economic and ethical reasons.

Any complex blob of life is interesting. The rhinoceros, blue whale, panther, whooping crane, mountain gorilla, orchid, ant – each evokes a distinct image, a sharp response, that does not need to be garnished with adjectives. If any of these animals became extinct the world would be a poorer place. Given the power to change, to develop industry, agriculture, transport or any other human activity, we should exercise the responsibility to curb those tendencies – ignorance, greed, or apathy – which lead to senseless waste.

Unfortunately this argument is not beyond challenge, as Myers reminds us. Even human life is a tradeable commodity – every year over a quarter of a million people die on the world's roads, the acceptable price of rapid transportation. Most people would probably welcome the extinction of smallpox, tapeworms and tsetse fly. These could be justified as convenient losses. After all, 95% of all the species that have ever lived have become extinct. The one absolute value is the survival of life on earth. In Tennessee a few years ago a small fish, the Tennessee Snail Darter, was sacrificed for a dam project. In this case the immediate effects of the Darter's extinction were not obviously noticeable – the rest of Tennessee's river life survived the loss. The problem humanity must solve is that species are disappearing so rapidly because of human development that local, regional and eventually global ecosystems will irretrievably break down. We must change.

Not surprisingly, the most effective arguments for saving wild species are those which demonstrate how humanity benefits from their survival. In general terms wild animals and plants provide many of the basic ingredients – food, firewood, shelter, clothing, medicine, income – upon which the survival of hundreds of millions of people depends. Sixty-two countries obtain 20% or more of their average daily per capita supply of animal protein from wild species, and of these 19 obtain 50% or more. Between 70–80% of the population of developing countries use traditional medicines culled from the wild. In First World countries routine injections of genes, synthesized chemicals, and raw materials derived from wild species are essential for the continued development of agriculture, industrial output and medicine. Wheat, rice, maize and potatoes contribute more food than the next 26 most important crops combined. Intensively grown as monocultures, each is extremely susceptible to disease, pests, or sudden changes in the climate. Regular cross-breeding with wild strains is essential to maintain or increase crop yields. Yet throughout the world wild strains are disappearing, literally in tens of thousands, from their original centres of origin – e.g. Bolivia, Colombia, Ethiopia, Mexico, and the Middle East.

The potential benefits of wild strains are enormous: IR36 was the first rice cultivar with resistance to all four major Asian rice pests and all four major Asian rice diseases; much of this resistance originated from a single sample of wild rice (*Oryza nivara*) found only in central India. Tomatoes, coffee, cotton, pineapples, rubber, bananas, cassava, cocoa – there is a lengthy list of commercial plant crops similarly dependent (see *What's Wildlife Worth?*, further reading).

The World Health Organisation has identified over 100 biologically active plant species from which essential drugs can be produced. Of these 43 are only available from the wild. Over 25% of prescriptions in the United States contain ingredients from higher plants. Many animals provide vital contributions to the development of new medicines – bee venom is used to combat arthritis, cotton-topped marmosets have helped produce a potent anti-cancer vaccine, and the Florida manatee potentially holds a key to haemophilia.

Industry, too, has harvested its fair share of the world's wild wealth. Rubber, gums, resins, oils, dyes, leathers, glues *et al.* are typical examples of commercialised crops. Global demand for natural rubber is escalating as oil prices force the cost of synthetic rubber upwards. The guayule shrub is expected to meet much of this increased demand in the future – up to one quarter of the plant consists of rubber, and every ton produced yields half a ton of valuable resin for gums and oils, as well as 25 kg of hard wax with one of the highest known melting points (76°C).

As might be expected, tropical forests have yielded other treasures. The babussu palm produces a fruit like a coconut but contains 72% more oil for use in soap, detergents, and starches. The leftover seed cake makes a high protein animal feed while the husk can be turned into charcoal. The tropical copaiba tree produces 20 litres of diesel-like heavy oil every six months, which reportedly can be poured straight into diesel engines.

There are, then, compelling reasons to advocate pragmatic exploitation. But, complications again lurk around the corner. Use often turns into abuse. Chimpanzees (for hepatitis B), the African Green monkey (for poliomyelitis vaccine) and South American owl monkey (for malaria chemo-therapy studies) are all used extensively in medical research institutes, as are many other species of primates. The US imported 34,000 primates in 1977 from tropical moist forests. This heavy demand has contributed to the decline of wild primates. There are only about 50,000 chimpanzees left in the wild, and India banned exports of wild rhesus monkeys in 1977 to protect severely diminished populations. Even captive-bred primates only relieve the pressures on wild species; they cannot solve all the problems. *Is* it right to breed such highly evolved creatures specifically for experimentation? The animals rights movement categorically condemns such proposals. Any use inevitably involves value judgements. Conservationists could be forgiven for throwing up their hands in despair of ever resolving these problems. But then 'perfect solutions' in any area are usually illusory. What is important is to begin applying remedies.

*   *   *

The World Conservation Strategy, basking in a precise utilitarian analysis, sets forward three objectives for conservation. To protect the biosphere, the thin mantle of soil, water and air that contains and sustains life, we must (1) maintain essential ecological processes and support systems, (2) preserve genetic diversity, and (3) use species and ecosystems on a sustainable basis. All of which are at least in principle hard to oppose, even for politicians and developers. Most governments can claim they have tried to plan for conservation. Every nation can boast of laws and regulations curbing the activities of individuals and institutions which detrimentally affect wild species and their habitats. On an international level, the number and scope of conventions and agreements to conserve grows almost yearly (a measure that we are reaching the planet's natural limits) – the Convention on International Trade in Endangered Species (signed by 81 countries), the Convention on Antarctic Marine Living Resources, the World Heritage Convention, the Convention on Migratory Species, and the RAMSAR Convention on Wetlands of International Importance are some of the best known. However, no matter how carefully framed, well-intentioned or supported in principle, so many words on so many bits of paper are just that. Brazil, for instance, which controls 33% of all tropical moist forests, has passed a radical law to protect its dwindling forest reserves. Any landowner is forbidden to clear more than 50% of his holding. Which sounds fine, except that nothing prevents the land being sold to someone else, who can clear 50% of the remaining forest. And so on.

The International Whaling Commission (IWC) perhaps most clearly demonstrates how a group of nations can act in concert, ostensibly to use a living natural resource sustainably, and end up by decimating what are arguably the world's most magnificent creatures. Established in 1946, the International Convention for the Regulation of Whaling was signed by 14 countries to safeguard the 'great natural resources represented by the whale stocks' for future generations. The Convention recognised this type of conservation was in the common interest of all members and noted that previous over-whaling 'in one area after another' made it 'essential to protect all species of whales from further over-fishing'.

If the independent activities of the main whaling nations – the UK, USA, Norway, Australia, South Africa and Iceland amongst others – before the Second World War left much to be desired, the later combined efforts of the IWC managed to maximise stupidity and cynical over-exploitation. The lessons of earlier years were deliberately ignored. The collapse of the Atlantic humpback stocks in just seven years between 1910 and 1918, and decimation of the blue whale stocks between the late 1920s and early 1930s, were two clear examples of spectacular mismanagement. The catch figures graphically tell the story: in 1910 some 6000 humpbacks were killed; in 1913 over 13,000 were taken; and by 1918 kills had plummeted to under 400. Blue whales were similarly decimated with the catch in 1932 of c. 30,000 falling to an almost unbelievably low figure of c. 7000 by the next year.

In this respect the post-war IWC supported the long-held traditions of whaling. Despite repeated recommendations from its Scientific Committee to reduce or halt the killing of blue and humpback whales, member countries continued to take full quotas. Even when the IWC agreed to stop limited hunting, those whaling nations affected by the ban simply registered official objections, a legal manoeuvre which, under the rules of the IWC, allowed whaling to continue unimpeded. After all, blue and humpbacks were important. Big (blue whales grow up to 150 tonnes with veins large enough for a child to crawl through) and slow, both species gave the highest catch per unit effort, the industry's measure of efficiency. Inevitably blue and humpback populations crashed, becoming commercially extinct. Subsisting at a fraction of original levels, 4% (3–4,000) and 6% (5,000) respectively, neither species has recovered despite an enforced ban on all killing since the mid 1960s. Unperturbed, the whalers simply switched to other species; primarily the fin, sei, sperm, and eventually, the smallest commercially hunted baleen whale, the minke, as other stocks gave out. Repeatedly condemned for failing to control over-hunting, for ignoring scientific advice to protect and conserve, and for basing quotas on speculative assumptions, the IWC has presided over the decimation of most commercially hunted whale stocks.

Even the establishment of the New Management Procedure in 1975, whereby allowable catches were to be calculated strictly in accordance with scientific assessments of each stock, proved of little help. It was not until 1982 that it was finally admitted that the basis for such assessments – a comprehensive understanding of whale population dynamics – could not be calculated. Even the most sophisticated biological models could only establish guidelines for stocks which were already depleted!

Bowing to unprecedented international pressure, stoked by the voluntary conservation movement and the increasing concern of some IWC members committed to the rescue of a global resource, the IWC at last agreed, in 1982, to phase out commercial whaling within three years. However, three countries – Japan, USSR, and Norway – are, at present, determined to continue. All have lodged objections.

Although commercial whaling is the most significant threat, it is not the only one. The most endangered species of great whale, the bowhead, is at risk of extinction because of aboriginal whaling. Pursuing their cultural right to hang on to a way of life established over centuries, the Alaskan Innuit continue to kill bowheads by traditional methods – waiting silently for days on end at the edge of the pack-ice, ready to slip out in small boats to harpoon their quarry as the whales migrate along the coast. Yet with probably less than 3,500 bowheads remaining, and a meagre replacement rate of between 60–70 animals a year, even the Innuit's small quotas are a grave threat to the bowhead's survival. For years conservationists have been torn between supporting the rights of native peoples and trying to prevent the extinction of an irreplaceable living creature.

*   *   *

As with any other commodity, scarcity forces the price up. In 1978 a single blue whale was worth over £100,000. Pirate whalers operating illegally outside the proscriptions of the IWC, rushed in where more reputable operations feared to tread. By 1980 rogue ships were killing an estimated 10,000 whales a year – many highly endangered – regardless of protection status, age, size or sex. The whaling authorities stood by, impotent and unheeding. Finally the pirates were stopped when conservationists, acting independently, sank three vessels (one rammed, two mined).

The escalation of the market value of any species spurs the trade, which further endangers it. In the Far East, rhino horn, treasured for magical and spurious medicinal purposes, rose in value over 20 times between 1975 and 1980. Similarly, between 1950 and 1978 the price of ivory rose 89 times, far faster than that of gold. The tally of black rhino, the most numerous variety, has fallen from tens of thousands in Africa to under 15,000 in barely 10 years. In 1975 there were roughly four million African elephants; in 1982 there were 1.3 million. Like the blue whale, both these species were the victims of greedy hunters, determined poachers and the illegal trade in their products.

In Japan leopard skin coats cost over $50,000; highly endangered bird species, such as the scarlet macaw, can fetch up to $15,000. In the US, varieties of rare plants such as exotic orchids command similar prices. The temptation to kill animals for the sake of their by-products is hard for some people to resist. The level of trade is staggering – the traffic in wildlife products amounted to $1,000,000,000 in 1981. The US, Europe and Japan are the largest markets. Each year it is estimated that 500,000 spotted and striped cats, two million crocodiles and up to 10 million birds are killed or sold.

The Convention on International Trade in Endangered Species (CITES) takes as its premise the lowest common denominator theory – preventing extinction. Its primary purpose is to monitor and regulate the wildlife trade by means of a licensing system common to all member nations. Commercial trade in critically endangered species is prohibited; threatened species can only be traded under a licence issued by the country of origin. Although CITES has improved considerably since its inception in 1973, its difficulties are typical of other conservation agreements. Enforcement, lack of information, and conditional acceptance of its restrictions by member nations are serious weaknesses. The largest wildlife centres, such as Thailand and Singapore, have yet to sign the Convention. These free ports offer little or no controls on either the kind or volume of traffic they encourage. Smuggled species are often 'laundered' by traders issuing forged licences, confusing the country of origin. In 1980 ocelot, otter and crocodile skins worth £5 million were illegally imported into West Germany from Paraguay. The export permits were fakes. Finally, many members of CITES table reservations against the bans on particular species products, which allows them to continue trading, in much the same way as the 'let-out' clause allows IWC members to ignore restricted quotas of whales.

Despite these drawbacks CITES is proving in many ways the most effective international agreement to protect wild species. At the last meeting in Botswana in 1983 delegates resisted attempts to relax restrictions on the trade in products of wolves, bobcats, lynx, otter, small ivory products and cacti. Although Canada's lobbying defeated proposals to regulate the trade in harp and hooded seals, the remaining species of great whales, including the Minke, Bryde's and four bottlenose varieties were accorded the highest form of protection in the face of tough opposition from Japan, Peru, Brazil and the Soviet Union. Equally significant were proposals to investigate the farming or ranching of wild species, including endangered and threatened ones, as a means of continuing trade and simultaneously ensuring its survival.

Papua New Guinea is exempt from the ban on commercial trade in the saltwater crocodile, a highly endangered species. A successful conservation scheme encourages captive breeding in a network of some 100 village farms. The 10% of the crocodile population in captivity earns $2 million of foreign exchange annually, employs hundreds of people and supplies vital protein. The savannah plains of East Africa offer a similar potential to farm wild ungulates, many of which have inbred genetic advantages over domestic animals as range species. Antelope, such as Thomson's gazelle, multiply rapidly and become sexually mature at an early age, and the Cape Eland will graze at night when the water content of the desert grasses is up to 40% higher. In other parts of the world turtles, butterflies and fur-bearing species are bred for their products.

If conservation is to work, the needs of animals must be matched to a large extent with those of people. Traditional solutions can cause as many problems as they solve. In Tanzania and Kenya large wildlife reserves, set aside by earlier generations as virgin wilderness, are under severe pressure to develop culling programmes of prolific species for meat and skins. In the next 20 years Kenya's population is expected to double, and yet 90% of its land is uncultivated. Its game reserves, the envy of the world, are naturally resented by the majority of the hard pressed local people. A pilot project is being considered, capable of processing up to 250,000 animals each year including elephants, giraffe, and wildebeest. Some animal populations have proliferated to such an extent that they now exceed the carrying capacity of the land. In Serengeti Park wildebeest have expanded twenty fold, to over two million animals, in under 30 years. Zimbabwe has already begun culling elephants in an attempt to control soaring numbers and protect the original habitat – by 1986 up to 12,000 will be shot in Hwange National Park alone.

As artificial environments are created to conserve wild creatures, in these cases by the national park boundaries, it is unavoidable that human management will take over from natural selection as the means to maintain a balance between competing populations. The tragedy would be if species already endangered came under further threat from the by-products of the culls of specific prosperous populations. Without strict safeguards, the sale of elephant ivory from Zimbabwe, one of the few countries where the elephant is rising in numbers, could undermine controls on other ivory stocks.

*   *   *

The more stable and resilient a natural system is, the greater its species' diversity. Despite the success of zoos and other captive breeding centres in rescuing a handful of species from extinction – Pere David's deer, the okapi and the Arabian oryx, for instance – the only reliable method of guaranteeing variety and stability is by protecting wild habitats and ecosystems. To ensure the permanent survival of a captive stock at least 100 individuals must be collected, one half of which should be from the wild. A survey of the world's zoos in 1971 revealed that only eight mammals met this criterion.

National parks are the traditional way of protecting species in their natural environment. At present under 2% of the earth's land is listed as wildlife reserves. Many of its 200 distinct biogeographic zones are not covered by any protection. And in most cases present reserves are too small. Since 1979 Brazil, for instance, has established a network of national parks, biological reserves and ecological stations covering 10,143,263 ha or 2.04% of Amazonia. The national plan, drawn up primarily by Brazilian Forestry agencies, gives priority to ecosystem protection. However, it is founded almost entirely on plant, as opposed to animal, diversity. Consequently it does not safeguard many areas of high species endemicity, where unusually large concentrations of wild fauna are found. These areas are believed to be Pleistocene forest refuges, isolated during the last cold dry climate at the end of the Quarternary era some 21,000–13,000 years BC. They are often bounded by rivers, which limit the distribution of many primate, mammal, bird, butterfly, as well as plant, species. If Brazil's National Park network is to be effective these forest refuges need to be safeguarded. As isolated biological islands, reserves, no matter how well planned, run the risk of becoming living museums, where stable wildlife populations are increasingly difficult to sustain. For instance, it is estimated that in the larger African parks one-twentieth of large mammals will disappear in 50 years, one quarter in 500 years and three-quarters in 5,000 (for the smaller parks corresponding figures are one-quarter, two-thirds and nine-tenths). While the United States boasts the greatest number of protected natural areas (which are currently under attack from its exploitative Republican Administration) and many developing countries, notably Costa Rica, Zambia, Cameroon, Venezuela and Zaire, are establishing extensive park networks, global environmental protection will only become effective when development is grounded in conservation, as recommended by the World Conservation Strategy. Ill-conceived and inappropriate development, whether of capital projects or human populations, represent the greatest threats to wild species.

Tropical moist forests illustrate this most clearly. Trees grow. They seed and grow again, and again. In this respect they are unlike oil or other non-renewable resources. This any child knows, and logically, it should form the heart of any forest management programme. One might be forgiven for wondering what most tropical forest managers were thinking about as children. Consider a few facts: about 100,000 square kilometres of South and Central America are cleared each year – only one third of Central America's forest remain and will probably be gone within the next 20 years; in South-East Asia more than 150,000 square kilometres are levelled annually; in equatorial Africa more than one million km^2 have been removed (Eneas Salati and Peter Vose, 'Depletion of Tropical Rain Forests', *Ambio*, 12(2).)

There are roughly 900 million hectares of tropical moist forest left. Latin America contains 58%, Africa 19% and South-East Asia and Oceania 23%. Brazil alone possesses 33% of the total, an area three times the size of France. Tropical rainforests comprise two-thirds of all tropical moist forests; they are wetter than the remaining deciduous forests, with average rainfalls of between 160 and 400 inches per year. Although the range of soils is wide, most tropical moist forests (TMF) are based on virtually sterile soils (Java is an exception due to volcanic eruptions). However, TMF vegetation has evolved efficient methods for recycling the nutrient rich humus and other organic debris littering the forest floor. Root systems, for instance, usually spread laterally. When TMFs are cleared the nutrients quickly disappear, due to wind or water erosion, and the sterile soil is left.

The reasons for felling are varied: there is therefore no simple solution. Deforestation due to slash-and-burn clearance for shifting agriculture, where the land is cleared and cropped for two or three seasons before the cultivator moves on, accounts for some 200,000 km^2 of secondary forestry degradation and perhaps one third of primary rainforest loss. Nigeria and the Ivory Coast are particularly affected, and both Indonesia and Brazil have encouraged colonisation of tropical rainforests by migrant settlers who have quickly exhausted the poor soils exposed from the forest. Over 70% of the two billion extra people expected by the end of the century will be born in developing countries. Feeding, housing and meeting their needs will inevitably put great pressure on the remaining tropical forests.

The commercial value and homogeneity of South-East Asia's dipterocarp (with their 'two-winged' fruit, tall straight trunks and few branches) tree species has caused intensive logging by international and national forestry companies. After 20 years many Asian forests are on the verge of commercial extinction. In Indonesia log production multiplied more than sixfold between the period 1961–65 (4.1 million cubic metres) and 1976–79 (25.9 million cubic metres). In the Philippines, traditionally a major timber exporter, forests now cover only 30% of the country (Tropical Moist Forests, Catherine Caufield, Earthscan 1982). Most logging involves highly selective use of tree species, with the majority being burnt or degraded during extraction. Laws requiring reafforestation or limited felling in many countries are usually ignored, and most logging companies prefer to finish their extraction as rapidly as possible, rather than establish long-term sustainable management programmes. They argue that unpredictable governments and economic instability forces this course. Where clearfelling takes place the land usually reverts to semi-scrub or will take hundreds of years to regenerate.

Japanese and US multinational forestry companies are primarily responsible for tropical deforestation in South-East Asia and Australia. Japan, in particular, has embarked on an expansionist forestry policy dependent on high volume imports as a way of protecting its own forests. Consequently, Japan has over 68% of its original forest cover intact, and countries like Thailand are now net importers of forestry products.

Paupa New Guinea (PNG) illustrates what often happens. Home of 33 out of the 43 known species of birds of paradise, the world's largest butterfuly, the Queen Alexandra birdwing, and the world's largest pigeon, the crested blue gowra, PNG has a remarkably diverse wildlife, most of which is dependent on the tropical rain forest. By 1990, the remaining commercially accessible forest will be committed for development. Although virtually all land is privately owned, the Government has purchased timber rights for large areas. Seventy-five per cent of all timber products are exported, the bulk of which go in an unprocessed state to Japan. Japan also owns over half the available forestry concessions on PNG. Despite this high level of involvement, PNG is only the ninth largest supplier of timber to Japan.

The problems that PNG face in using their forests sustainably are typical of most tropical forest countries. For example, according to the Fourth Malaysia Plan, prepared by the Malayan government, while 119,250 acres of former forests were replanted between 1971 and 1980, annual exploitation averaged 900,000 acres per year. Although reafforestation is now written into timber agreements, enforcement is extremely difficult. Replanting is poorly carried out (usually at about 10% of clearfell rates) using monoculture varieties (pine or eucalypts) that are no ecological substitutes for the original forest cover. In PNG there are over 500 native tree species.

Apart from the lack of reafforestation to replace the resource, companies also fail to establish processing facilities, thereby creating jobs and preventing the export of profits with the unprocessed logs. Moreover, multinational timber companies are known to misrepresent amounts and varieties of log exports deliberately, to avoid tax-duty, and to exploit transfer pricing policies. Under these schemes multinationals with vertically-integrated timber industries set up specialist subsidiaries. These often have high debt-to-equity ratios with consequently high interest payments going back to the overseas parent company. Products are then sold between the companies at advantageous i.e. low profitmaking prices. Both practices enable the companies to avoid taxes and export duties. Consequently the revenue-generating capacity of the forests is literally exported with the wood, giving little relief to the hard pressed economies of the tropical forest nations, who then intensify further use of the forests. Long-term forestry agreements, a need for the roads and employment provided by the forestry companies, and inadequate government policies, where the incentive is to sell to raise income in the short term, all help prevent effective and rational forestry use.

Finally, roads, cattle ranching and mining also contribute to extensive deforestation. More than a quarter of all Central American forests have been destroyed since 1960 to produce beef for lean meat hamburgers. Almost 40% of all deforestation in Brazil has been due to cattle ranching. This is the worst possible use of tropical rainforests, as the land becomes exhausted after 5–7 years. Roads open up the forests to migrant settlers and cultivators. In India the construction of a dam in Panshet resulted in the surrounding hill regions being deforested as logging operators exploited the newly-created accessibility. Although the Brazilian Transamazonian highway has not been completed, finished sections have resulted in large influxes of people, the introduction of diseases to which native peoples are particularly susceptible, and subsequently degradation of forest life.

The Amazon basin has major deposits of bauxite, tin ore, kaolin, manganese and gold as well as the world's largest known iron reserves at Serra dos Carajos. Peru, Bolivia and Indonesia have other high-quality mineral deposits. All are additional incentives to clear and burn the forest cover.

The ecological effects of deforestation are cumulative. Land failure and drastic changes in land use lead to reduced infiltration rates, increased water run-off on newly-cleared soils, extensive flooding in lowland areas and soil erosion. In West Africa run-off is as much as 20 times greater from cultivated soil as from forest areas; the loss of soil is 6,300 times as great. India loses 6,000 million tonnes of soil by erosion every year, along with plant nutrients equivalent to twice the country's annual fertiliser production. The consequences – annual famine, flash floods and repeated crop failure – for poor, large rural populations are literally overwhelming. Felling forests for firewood in the slopes of the Himalayas has resulted in these disasters being regularly inflicted on millions of peoples living in the mountains' catchment areas.

Globally, the loss of tropical moist forests may have an even more serious result – known as 'the greenhouse effect'. One estimate supposes that if half the carbon in the Amazon were released over the next 20 years, and half remained in the atmosphere, carbon dioxide levels would rise by roughly 5%. This may be sufficient to increase global temperature levels by 2–3° Centigrade, due to the thermal infrared radiation absorption of CO^2. Such a temperature rise could cause partial melting of the North Atlantic and West Antarctic ice sheets with consequent flooding of low-lying coastal areas. Similarly, large-scale deforestation may affect the climate by interfering with the atmospheric heat balance, as less solar energy is absorbed by the dwindling forest cover ('Depletion of Tropical Rain Forests', ibid.). The effect on atmospheric circulation if tropical rainforests are removed over equatorial Africa, America and Asia is unknown. As the prospects do not seem bright, why risk finding out the hard way?

*   *   *

The conventional treatment of tropical moist forest is a classic example of ill-conceived development which ignores even notional requirements of sustainability. But sustainable use, although a convenient and practical baseline from which to gauge interference with the natural state of things, is only one criterion. It is not always appropriate. There are other considerations. Antarctica provides a case in point.

Antarctica's abundant wild life includes critically endangered cetaceans like the blue, pigmy blue, fin, sei, humpback and Southern right, as well as more common minke, Southern bottle-nosed, long-finned pilot whales and several dolphin species. The crabeater (estimated population 30 million) is the most numerous seal, followed by the Weddell (1 million), Southern elephant (600,000), Southern fur (500,000), Ross (200,000) and leopard (200,000). The 1972 Convention on Antarctic seals was drawn up to regulate future hunting of seal species – so far no nation has shown an interest, although the USSR took 1,000 crabeaters experimentally in 1971–2. Habitat destruction and the disturbance of breeding beaches by oil and mineral exploiters are far more serious threats.

Over one hundred species of fish have been discovered, and there are seven dominant bird families including penguins, albatrosses, skuas and gulls. Little is known of their breeding or feeding habits. Nevertheless, commercial interests are never far away. In 1982, a Japanese company was refused permission by Argentina, after a huge international outcry, to kill 48,000 magellan penguins to make soft leather gloves.

The Southern Ocean is the foundation of Antarctica's teeming wildlife. Here three major water masses continually circulate, creating a rich soup of carbon dioxide, oxygen and nutrients from which spawn masses of phytoplankton, the main food supply of krill, a shrimp-like crustacean, and other zooplankton. Between parallels 57°S and 63°S is a physical transition zone, known as the Convergence. Here surface water, incorporating freshly-melted ice and snow, a warm deep water layer, which is very salty, high in carbon dioxide and originates in the major northern oceans, meets and mixes with Antarctica bottom water, which is also salty and high in oxygen.

The complex system of currents and upwellings ideally suit the primary krill species, *Euphasia superba*, whose enormous populations are the cornerstone of the entire Antarctic marine ecosystem. One recent swarm discovered near Elephant Island measured over 10,000 tonnes, a seventh of the world fish catch. Total numbers have been put as high as 1,350 million tonnes, although reasonably reliable acoustic surveys now estimate the standing stock at 650 million tonnes. Krill is the primary food source of five species of whale, three of seal, twenty of fish, three of squid and numerous species of sea bird. Also, killer and sperm whales, Weddell and Ross seals, and Emperor penguins, for instance, feed on fish and cephalopods, which in turn eat krill. Now, however, krill stocks are increasingly regarded as alternatives to depleted fisheries. Baleen whales, including the highly-endangered blue, humpback and Southern right, would be especially vulnerable to any interference with krill stocks. A substantial krill fishery could severely jeopardise their ever more remote chances of recovery. To make matters worse, any commercial fishery will occur in open seas during the short summer months, in direct competition with feeding whales and other marine animals.

Many deep sea fishing nations, notably Russia, Japan, South Korea and Poland, are barred from traditional fishing grounds under 200-mile Exclusive Economic Zones. Antarctic waters are the obvious replacement. In 1979, the total krill harvest amounted to some

200,000 tonnes. By 1982 USSR alone was reported to have caught one million tonnes of fin fish and krill. The USSR has 200 trawlers operating in Antarctic waters, and Japan is presently building a fleet of super trawlers especially for Antarctic fishing grounds. Some scientists estimate that the annual sustainable yield of krill could equal the present catch from the rest of the world, but most reasonable estimates put the total potential catch at no higher than two million tonnes. At present we do not know enough about the life cycle, reproductive rates, feeding or swarming behaviour of krill, or its interactive relations with other species, to allow large catches. For many years it was thought that minke whale and crabeater seal populations had expanded to fill the ecological niche created by depleted whale species. However, this is no longer thought to be the case.

Some scientists argue that these whale populations will never recover until competing species approach former levels; others question the assumptions underlying the 'vacuum' theory. Whichever is eventually proved right, the whales are in a precarious state. A 1981 survey by the IWC spotted only 17 humpbacks and seven blue whales in Antarctic waters. Without detailed information about the biodynamics of marine populations, any exploitation should be considered inconceivable.

The Convention of Antarctic Marine Living Resources was drawn up in 1980 in order to avoid this sort of confusion. The boundaries of the Convention are marked by the Antarctic Convergence; within its limits, the signatories are required to adopt an 'ecosystem' approach, through a biological model, whereby any proposed use is curbed by its effect on other species. This unique safeguard, a first in international law and grounded on the principles of the World Conservation Strategy, was designed specifically to prevent the over-exploitation and collapse of any trophic level in Antarctica's fragile, short food chains. Sadly, these good intentions have so far amounted to little. Under the Convention any decision must be ratified by consensus, a system which would appear to work equally well for conservationists as exploiters. But, unlike the IWC, there are no obvious conservationist countries in the Convention. Control of Antarctica's marine resources is established firmly amongst its members, all of whom have an interest in exploitation. None seem prepared to make the biological approach work. At one recent meeting in Hobart, observers condemned the repeated blocking of management plans designed to prevent over-exploitation. Agreement was not even possible over the presentation of research to the Scientific Committee. The ghost of the IWC hovers in the wings.

The working or non-working of the Convention is a symptom of a deeper malaise overshadowing Antarctica. Since 1959, all human activities on the continent have been determined by the Antarctic Treaty, which formally established the peaceful harmony of scientific co-operation that has graced events until recently.

In 1973, the US oil exploration vessel, the Glomar Challenger, found positive traces of hydrocarbons in the Ross Sea continental shelf. Since 1981, the Japan National Oil Corporation has conducted extensive seismic surveys in the Bellinghausen Sea. West Germany, France and Australia are carrying out similar activities to probe Antarctica's extensive oil and mineral riches. Proposals from oil companies to carry out seismic searches have so far been postponed. All such operations seriously undermine, if they do not directly violate, agreements protecting Antarctica. While research carried out for scientific purposes is permitted, commercial exploration is not. Until now, all explorations by national governments have been technically justified as scientific research, despite obvious commercial implications.

The Antarctic Treaty side-lined all matters concerning mineral developments in the belief that they would exacerbate the conflicting territorial claims of the original signatories. Argentina, Australia, Chile, France, Norway, New Zealand and the United Kingdom formally claim territory in Antarctica. Some claims, particularly those of Argentina and the UK, overlap. Belgium, Japan, South Africa, the USA and the USSR, as well as Poland and West Germany, who acceded in 1977 and 1981 respectively, have made no formal claims. As a compromise Article 4 of the Treaty also sets aside territorial disputes, in effect putting them on ice. Although the Treaty has no expiry date, a review is possible after 1991 if any party requests it. It is certain that such a review will now take place, as economic incentives to develop override other considerations. Consultative parties to the Treaty have always formed an exclusive 'Club'. All meetings are held in secret session and the rights of other nations to determine the future of this global resource are steadfastly and consistently ignored. Internal disagreements are suppressed in order to stonewall outside 'interference'. But other countries are becoming increasingly aggravated by the attitude of the Club; some, like Malaysia, for reasons of conservation, others, like India, to claim a share of resources which most nations feel are not the prerogative of a few developed countries. Consequently the Treaty parties are racing to secure a working Minerals Regime (under which any company with sponsorship from a Treaty nation can apply for permission to explore for specific minerals) before third countries can block any agreement, most likely through the United Nations.

Future prospects are gloomy. Argentina has always maintained an unofficial military presence on her bases and Britain continues to fortify the Falklands. None of the Treaty nations is prepared to support a moratorium on development, even though environmental safeguards are impossible to guarantee. In the coldest, windiest and driest climate on earth, it is inevitable that an oil spill will occur once drilling has begun. Because of the sensitivity of marine species, particularly planktonic crustacea, the absence of oil-oxidising bacteria in the waters and the retardation of wave-assisted dispersal by ice floes, any oil spill would have disastrous long-term effects on the entire marine ecosystem.

Blow-outs in temperate waters, where working conditions are much kinder, are often unmanageable. In 1978 the Amoco Cadiz sank off Brittany; oil pollution severely affected marine systems over 150 km east of the disaster. Economies of scale and the advantages of ice-breaking will lead to supertankers of up to half a million tonnes being used in Antarctica. The Campeche I Ixtoc oilwell 'blow' in the mild Gulf of Mexico poured out over 300,000 tonnes of oil for 295 days. It required 14 planes and helicopters, over 500 workers and 22 ships to control; co-ordination on a similar scale would be well nigh impossible in Antarctica. The effects of one accident, magnified by ocean currents and climatic conditions, on krill swarms, baleen whales, sea birds and coastal penguin rookeries is unthinkable. Moreover, Antarctic oil pollution, spread by deep ocean currents, would degrade fishery and coastal zones as far as the Northern hemisphere. The technology does not exist to overcome these natural hazards. The welcome effects of the Treaty Parties in drawing up 'Agreed measures for the conservation of Fauna and Flora' in Antarctica will not compensate for these glaring deficiencies.

Cost is likely to inhibit future commercial development significantly. Only 2% of the continent is visible land. The rest is covered by a slowly moving sheet of ice over a mile thick on average: a formidable natural barrier. Although there are over 50 research stations on Antarctica, many scientists assert that significant development is hypothetical. Existing maps which purport to show large areas of potential hydrocarbon fields, coal deposits in the Trans-antarctic Mountains and platinum, gold, silver, copper, nickel and other minerals are misleading. Most of these are indicated solely on the basis of trace elements found in routine rock analysis. There is a probable tenfold increase in costs between a routine scientific research and useful prospecting surveys. Another tenfold cost increase would follow to prove the definite existence of a commercially viable resource. Nevertheless this pursuit of non-renewable and inaccessible resources continues. Britain, the US, the USSR, and India have all recently increased their budgets for Antarctic research.

If some Treaty members press their territorial claims hard, and the compromises built into the Antarctic Treaty break down, it is highly likely that the USA and the USSR will file independent claims, greatly adding to the difficulties between competing interests. The fisheries and mineral potential, the mounting claims of third countries, the growing interests of conservationists and the persistent intransigence of the 'Club' all add fuel to the flames. In such circumstances something other than a way of dividing resources and sorting out development priorities, even if they are intended to be sustainable and equitable, is required.

In 1982, the 10th anniversary of the Stockholm Conference, environmentalists gathered in Nairobi and passed a resolution calling upon the Antarctic Treaty nations to establish Antarctica as a World Park. Similar calls to recognise the continent's status as a protected global commons were made in 1972 when representatives from over 80 countries met in the US to consider the worldwide national park system, in 1975 when New Zealand proposed dropping her own territorial claims, and in 1982 at the 3rd World Conservation Parks Conference in Bali. Even the utilitarian World Conservation Strategy recognises exceptions can be made to the rule of always using resources, in its support for a halt to commercial whaling. The case for Antarctica to be treated comparably is compelling.

Controls on the treatment of wild creatures, such as preventing the hunting of endangered species or looking after the species we use, make conservation work. But the most effective action we can take to roll back the inexorable development policies set in motion by previous generations, and spurred on by the present one, lies in safeguarding wild habitats. This cannot be achieved by designating a few precious sites as 'natural areas', isolated from surrounding environments where man and beasts battle for supremacy. That drama is doomed to have a tragic ending. What we need is a systematic network of protected areas, including both representative samples and unique types of primary ecosystems, spread throughout the world. Special measures must be taken to safeguard those regions which harbour the greatest concentrations of endemic species, such as the pleistocene tropical forest refuges. Immediate attention must be given to those areas in this category which are currently under threat, like Madagascar, the mountain forests of East Africa, or Brazil's northwestern tropical forests.

The commonsense priorities of the World Conservation Strategy, in particular grounding development in sustainable conservation, cannot be ignored. Wild species can better the lot of human beings if appropriate precautions are taken. But to direct the 'maximum sustainable yield' from a wild population is often little else than rationalising wanton greed. We have sufficient examples of grossly mismanaged populations – the great whales, North Sea herring, the American bison, the South African quagga – to see what happens if we are not careful. That surely is the message – to be full of care.

Because we recognise the sacrosanct quality of life does not automatically preclude us from capturing, killing, and using living things. It may well do for some individuals, but biological and physical necessities will ensure that it does not for larger societies. Conservationists should, therefore, try to be effective by doing two things: first, when recommending sustainable use, they should guard against the delusion that the entire planet can become a managed arena, where living things are regulated and manipulated according to rational principles; and second they should aim to treat wild places and wild creatures with respect, which may mean leaving them well alone.

Wild species and the places they inhabit are part of the common heritage of the planet in which, like it or not, we all share. As the dominant species, we have a collective responsibility for doing our utmost, using whatever justification is most appealing or persuasive, to protect our wild neighbours, wherever they may occur. International wildlife conservation must become a prerogative of all nations. The success of the populist 'Save the Whale' campaign has shown what can be done, even in the face of powerful and intransigent nations and exploitative corporations.

An inevitable corollary of Darwinian evolution is that continuity between animals and humans works both ways. As the Federation of American Scientists recognised in 1977, if we accept that we have evolved from 'lower' animals, then we must accept a spectrum of emotional and intellectual ability among those animals. We cannot pretend that our links are solely physical; preliminary experiences with dolphins and apes confirms this truth. It is a fact which inevitably confounds many prevailing attitudes towards wild creatures, but at the very least it points to a provocative future between 'us' and 'them'.

Further Reading

Barnes, James N. 1982, *Let's Save Antarctica*, Greenhouse Publications.

Caufield, Catherine 1982, *Tropical Moist Forests*, Earthscan.

Inskipp, Tim and Wells, Sue 1979, *International Trade in Wildlife*, Earthscan.

Myers, Norman 1980, *The Sinking Ark*, Pergamon Press.

Prescott-Allen, Robert and Christine 1982, *What's Wildlife Worth?*, Earthscan.

Tønnessen, J. N. and Johnsen, A. O. 1983, *The History of Modern Whaling*, Hurst Publications.

Index